Would the Real Church PLEASE Stand Up!

~

By Susan Greenfield

In Christ,

Susan Greenfield

Would the Real Church PLEASE Stand Up!
by Susan Greenfield

Printed in the United States of America

ISBN 978-1-60266-025-0
IBSN 1-60266-025-5

Unless otherwise indicated, Bible quotations are taken from the New International Version. Copyright © 1973, 1978, 1984 by International Bible Society.

www.xulonpress.com

Table of Contents

Introduction

My mission is to increase domestic violence awareness in the Christian churches of America. Baptist churches, especially Southern Baptist churches may be the most challenging, and the most important area to begin.

When have you ever heard information or a sermon that addressed domestic violence? You probably are somewhat uneducated on this topic. I was, but WHY? Domestic violence is so taboo, especially in the church. It is not about the whole "We are women, hear us roar", or about placing women above men. It is about helping women to be free from abuse behind the closed doors of their homes. Keep in mind, at times, the "victim" is male. If you need to replace the word "woman" with "man", that is fine. I am writing from a wife's perspective. Abuse can definitely occur in live-in and dating relationships also. Abuse is abuse and should <u>never</u> be tolerated. Unacceptable actions, behaviors, and/or words create an unhealthy atmosphere. It is not God's desire that His children live under these circumstances. Do not let my words turn you away from God or church. We live in a fallen world and things happen. My personal experience with domestic violence has only strengthened my relationship with God. God has blessed me and helped me in so many ways. I am not bitter. I have a fire burning within me to help set others free and I do not blame God at all. I thank Him for my new found healthy home and hope many others find the strength to run from danger. It is my prayer that sharing my experience will help women currently in violent homes as well as other Christians trying to minister to battered women.

Some situations or comments may be mentioned more than once to show that it affects many areas and may help to give some insight on different subjects. As I am writing, I am experiencing a timeline of events. I am writing at times in the present tense. If I say "it has been five months now", you will know what is happening as I write. You are getting the first hand encounter.

My Story

I refuse to see myself as a victim. I am a survivor. That not only means I'm alive physically, for which I am grateful, but also I'm no longer a prisoner in a violent home. My children are also survivors. They have a new chance at life, just like I do. Let me open the door for you so you can see what went on behind these closed doors. You see, I'm a minister's wife. Aren't ministers' wives supposed to protect their husbands at all costs? Isn't every wife? This is almost what I did. My children could have lost their mother at the violent hands of their father. You never know what goes on behind closed doors.

At the age of 15, I became a Christian. Many Sunday mornings, as my family of five went their own ways, I was with my neighbors at church to learn more about this new Savior. I was the odd ball in my family. I decided to be baptized at church camp rather than at my church. The week I was baptized, I met the man of my future dreams. His name was Steve. He was funny, attractive, outgoing, and called to be a minister. He was 16 and already preaching in local churches. I thought so much of this guy. I tried to get my best friend to take him to Prom. We talked on the phone off and on for about 2 years, but rarely saw each other. Towards the end of our senior year, we began dating. We believed God wanted us to marry. When I told my parents the news, they about flipped. I obeyed my parents and continued to respect them. However, I could not live with them any longer. Steve and I knew we were to marry. We also knew we were to stay pure and to avoid the appearance of evil. Living together was not an option. Long story short; the wedding date was moved up. Things with my parents got worse and the date was moved up again.

We were the perfect little family. At one point, Steve was working full time and in Bible College and I was working part-time and in a beauty college. At the same time, we volunteered with two different youth groups as youth leaders. I don't remember exactly when things got weird, but it was within our first year of marriage. Several episodes occurred, but as a baby Christian I knew marriage was forever and felt it was a woman's duty to be submissive. I had no one to turn to anyway. As I look back as a 27 year-old at my 18 year-old self, I should have known something was wrong with this picture. I actually did, but had no resources.

- He got angry about something and ripped my favorite jeans completely off my body. Of course he was sorry and said, "I'll buy another pair of jeans for you".

- Steve put his fist through the wall and said I should be glad it was not my face.

- He was enraged and drove recklessly on some back roads. The car went airborne. As we crashed back on to the ground, he began to tell me if the frame was damaged, it was my fault.

I can recall a handful of other instances from that time period. Then things were okay, other than the fact that I started to worry about everything. It was not just worry, but debilitating fear. That lasted about year or so.

While we were living in our fifth home, he was the pastor at the seventh church we attended together. He was pushed out of the pulpit at the small country church that we had just watched double in size. He did nothing to deserve this loss of his job. The church disposed of 50 pastors in its 80 years of existence. That is just a tradition they had. It was devastating. After three years of infertility, I was holding our seven week old son as we stepped out of the white church on the hill for the last time. That is when it began. He was unable to find a job that would pay the bills. I found work that almost paid the bills. It was one hour and fifteen minutes from home. It was "temporary" he said, as he stayed home with our son and worked on his school via distance education. I would come home from work, clean the house, cook, and beg and yell at him to get a job or at least help with the house. Then I would go to bed. I missed my baby tremendously. He said he was looking for a job. He also made sure I knew that housework was a woman's job. Six months later, we moved closer to my work. He told me how most men would say, "Get over it. Everyone commutes to their work place." This move gave me two extra hours or more at home with my baby every day. That helped a lot and I felt less torn between work and my child. My husband continued to say unkind things such as making fun of my not so skinny body, calling me a lesbian, and saying I was unfaithful. (All of which were untrue). He was stressed and depressed about the whole church thing so I just tried to ignore the many unkind words and harsh looks. One of our topics of conflict was having another child. I was hoping he would get a job before I got pregnant. Staying home with the children was very important to me. He would remind me that children are a blessing from God and that it was not Godly for me to not want that blessing right then. When our son was 14 months old, I got pregnant. I was surprised because it took a while to get pregnant the first time. Still the only one working, I became very ill and lost 15 pounds in five months from a severe case of morning sickness. To make matters more complicated, my health insurance would not cover the pregnancy and we couldn't afford to make cash payments to the doctor. We had to pay $900 down before they would see me.

Two or three months into the pregnancy, the first physical abuse began. At least, it was the first time that I can remember.

It was a Sunday morning in the fall of 2003, when my husband was a guest preacher for a church of about twenty people in the middle of nowhere. He was going to preach and then interview for the position as their pastor. I got myself and our son ready for church. I took our son and my husband's Bible and sermon out to the truck. I started the truck then locked the truck doors because Steve was very paranoid about the sex offender registered two blocks away. When I reached in the house door about five feet from the truck, I picked up Steve's suit coat and realized the other set of keys was not on the key rack. The blood drained from my face. A locksmith could get our baby out quickly, but how was my husband going to respond? He had been escalating recently and it was going to be bad. I told him the keys could not be too far and asked him to watch our son so I could find them. He told me I was a terrible mother, didn't deserve the child I was carrying, lazy, stupid, good for nothing, and many other words that don't need to be repeated. I could not get around him into the hallway to look for the keys, so I told him I was going to call a locksmith. With the lady still on the telephone, I ran really fast to the bedroom where I found the keys. As I ran through the kitchen towards the telephone, he grabbed me. He slapped me in the face. I said, "I found the keys." Just then, a kitchen chair flew across the floor into my leg. It bruised immediately. I got on the telephone and told the woman we didn't need a locksmith. I was hoping she would send the police instead. It was not a quiet ordeal. She heard what was going on. We got in the truck and were off to share the message of God's love. As we drove down the road, he repeatedly reached over our baby who had been crying, to push me up against the truck door. He would say, "Get out" and cuss and belittle me. Towards the end of the trip to church, I was looking up scriptures to help him finish the sermon on paper. It was a beautiful sermon. He preached on depression and Elijah being restored back into the service of God. Part of the way through the service, I took the wound up little witness to his daddy's anger outside, to run off his energy. As we reentered the church, there were a bunch of wet eyed people who told me how God used my husband to encourage them to hang in there. I will remember that day forever.

When I was five months along, my husband began working for an insurance company. I had health insurance and it covered pregnancy. I cut my work hours back to part-time and my health improved. My husband hated his job because he had to be on time and he hated authority of all kinds. He said if I would have stayed working full-time and stopped acting as if I was sick, he would not have to work a job he hated. My job was not the most fun job either. It was high stress and a headache. He demanded that I fix his breakfast and lunch before he left for work. He said I should do it out of love, but it was never acceptable to him. Often he would throw his lunch away and eat out because he made the money, so he could spend it. That was fine, but why not just eat out instead of acting like I couldn't pack a lunch right?

Three months after Steve started working, he said we were moving. I didn't want to move while pregnant again and felt it would be too much financial pressure. He said my hormones were talking and that women are not logical thinkers and have no right to push a man around. So, we moved into our seventh home. Immediately, we had sewage and plumbing problems. Somehow, that was my fault also. Everyday for a couple weeks, I carried buckets of water from the kitchen sink to the bathtub for Steve's morning bath and then would go wake him up like a little alarm clock. He would get up, yell and slam doors because the pair of underwear he wanted was not in his drawer and his shirt had a wrinkle on the pocket. So what if the sewage was backed up in the house? It was a woman's job to get it done. If all of his clothes were perfect, he would find something else to set him off.

Then our daughter was born. In his mind, there was definitely no compassion for a body that just birthed a child. He stayed in a rage because the house wasn't clean enough. He stayed home from work for a couple days to help the plumber. He helped me by telling me what to do. He would not allow anyone to help me with an infant and a two-year-old. He said his mom did it and I should be able to handle it also. He wouldn't allow anyone to help, but expected the house and children to be spotless. When I got home from the hospital our toilet wouldn't flush, tub wouldn't drain, clothes washer and dishwasher couldn't be used and I was still carrying buckets of water. He terrorized his family. One minute he would say I was a good mother, the next he was threatening to leave me and take the kids away because I wasn't submissive enough. He would push me around and grab me. He would make threats and say he hated me for no reason. I just tried harder to please him as I put a smile on my face. Once in a while, I would fight back. It only made him more agitated. He soon started telling me he was going to kill me. Steve would cycle as most abusers do. I felt so trapped. No one knew the prison in which the children and I lived. We were not allowed to go outside. We couldn't go for walks to get exercise, as he told me how fat I was. Supper was never what he wanted. I never got a break because he didn't trust anyone to take care of the children. That summer was not a good one to say the least. He started pushing me to have another baby again. I told him I didn't think my body could handle it. That was not a good enough reason. After a while, he backed off on that.

I pleaded with God every day to deliver us from my husband. Friends and family regularly said what a wonderful man he was. "Trapped" is the word that described my life and there were two precious babies that were seeing and hearing more than anyone will ever know. Was he going to have to kill me before God would rescue us? If I told anyone, they would not believe me. He would even tell me that he was the best husband I could ever find. I didn't believe that for a second. Maybe the worst?

In December of 2004, Steve took another ministry position after quitting his other job a month before. For one week, he was pleasant to live with. He was excited about doing God's work once more. The second week of his new job didn't go as well as the first. So, of course, his family took the brunt of it. I called a prayer line one really bad day. The woman said she should call the police. I talked with her and told her if the police show up, he will kill me. She said I should talk to the senior pastor. She just didn't understand the consequences like I did. Around this time, I was considering "disappearing" with the children. This would buy some time. I would dress Renee like a boy. Isaac couldn't change much. I would change my appearance as much as possible. Maybe we could live in a church's basement somewhere. I was so desperate to be safe and keep my children safe. The more I thought and prepared, the less realistic it seemed. I would get caught. No one would believe me… I HAD to be legal and have evidence. I started documenting dates abuse would occur for two reasons. 1. If he killed me, there would be a paper trail that would point to him. 2. If I got brave enough and had the opportunity to run, documentation may be helpful. By calling prayer lines, I got connected with an organization to help those in violent situations. God hooked me up with a counselor on the phone I could speak with regularly. Around Christmas time, I began a journal and put aside the one hundred dollars my grandparents gave us for Christmas. I was planning my escape and planning in great detail.

A few months later, I began to pray that God would tell people what was going on. He did! A friend asked me if he ever hit me. I told her the truth and she promised not to tell anyone. My husband noticed I was talking to her more than before. He started regularly accusing me of sleeping with her. This was just a manipulative way of driving me away from any support system. Another friend noticed something very innocent that I had said to her. I threw up a red flag and she caught it! I told her more details. She cried with me and was then the best Christian support I could have asked for.

I was emotionally ready to leave him, but my fear was that nobody else would believe me. At church, he was known as a "gentle giant". After all, he was 6'3" and 290 pounds. This means twice my size, plus some. I was not as well liked at church. I was always friendly and smiling. People did not dislike me, but my actions appeared snobbish. Steve wouldn't allow me to leave the children in the nursery, so I sat with them in the nursery rather than going into the sanctuary. People regularly told me that they could handle my children for one hour so I could go to church. I wanted to go, but couldn't. You should have seen me dragging an eight-month-old and a two-year-old into the restroom. It was a sight. The women in the nursery invited me many times to scrapbook with them. I wanted to, but had to make up excuses for that also since I wasn't allowed. Mother's Day Out- it was the same thing. This mother didn't get a break. I needed a break from my demanding, controlling, critical husband more than I did from my two toddlers. So, who looks crazy to the outsider's view? How can I prove that he is unsafe? I decided to record him. Two different recorders had poor sound quality. I had to be sneaky about everything. Finally, the third and most expensive recorder worked. I began my investigative work. It was risky business, but had to be done for the sake of my children. My counselor on the telephone said I didn't need to go through all the trouble to basically prove my case. My gut said my ducks better be in a row. I trusted my gut like my counselor encouraged me to do before. My "gut" might have been the Holy Spirit. A pastor of a friend helped me with the computer part of the recorder. God was in that situation also. I still do not even know this pastor's name.

We went on family vacation. I was very nervous about what might happen. The first part of the week was okay. The last day of vacation was on Sunday. We visited a church. I took cookies to keep the kids quiet. After a while, we had to leave the service because the children became restless. Keep their ages in mind-3 years 2 months and 14 months. Steve got very angry with me for "coddling" them and giving them cookies. We got in the car and all hell broke loose. I can use that phrase because I was there. Isaac said, "You're a bad daddy". He pulled into a parking spot and said, "I'll show you bad daddy". Somewhere in the mess of words, Steve said he would kill both Isaac and me if he turns out like a specific young man we know. As he got out of the car I said, "Be careful". I picked up my cell phone out of my purse to call the police. He settled down before he took Isaac behind the car where he apologized to him.

Soon, I learned where the shelters were for people who needed protection. The most dangerous time for a woman is when she is leaving. For over 3 months before I left, physical abuse was occurring every 8-10 days. It was a predictable cycle and didn't seem as though it would stop. I wanted so badly to believe my husband was not the typical batterer, but that a chemical imbalance was responsible for his behavior. Now, five months after leaving him, I see it is much more than a chemical imbalance. I do believe mental illness in some form is present. He still shows abusive behavior and still blames me for it. It still doesn't come out in front of other people either, which tells me he has some control over it.

Well, I continued making recordings and making plans. I had a survival box labeled "Baby Items" in our spare room to take when I left. He had two retreats planned with the youth group. I decided that would be the safest way to leave. He would be gone for a couple days. I was preparing to leave, but was scared to death.

He decided we were moving again. I did not disagree much with his plan. I took my "Baby Items" to a friend and told her I would be back within a couple months to retrieve it. I didn't want him to find my survival kit in the move. We moved. I was holding on to hope that he would feel more at ease in our home in the country. Of course, nothing changed. Three weeks later, he went on a retreat. That was when I decided to leave and my children and I were on our way to a shelter where the walls had metal sheets between the bricks and the windows had bars. Video cameras were everywhere. We were safe. That day, I felt that peace that comes only from our Heavenly Father. That day, I also called his mother so someone would be there to keep him from killing himself like he had frequently suggested. I went to the courthouse and got an emergency protection order, which he would later break repeatedly for what has been five months now.

The last three ½ years have been challenging, but I have to say that God has shown me His hand very regularly since leaving my home. He has given me His peace and taken care of us. My children are doing much better since living in a peaceful home. And those recordings, that is why a judge believed me. I have custody of the two biggest blessings I have ever seen.

This is the very condensed version. You should see my journal. Life is better now, but like the aftermath of a destructive storm, there is also the aftermath of domestic violence. I am currently facing challenges such as:

* Fear that my husband or his family will break into my home and hurt me when I am in the shower or when I am sleeping.
* Harassment by phone and when meeting for visitation for children.
* Filing police reports for violation of the protection order. (I made at least two trips to the police department before actually following through with it.)
* Finances.
* A night-light is not enough. A friend says my house is "lit up like a Christmas tree at night".
* Trying to help my children overcome what they have witnessed.
* When the children come home after being with their dad they are like different people. Disrupted sleep, anger,

fear, sadness, confusion, disobedience, uncontrollable crying, hypersensitivity.
* I am juggling the role of mom, dad, provider, home repairer, housekeeper, and trying to heal at the same time.

The purpose for sharing my story is not to obtain pity. That is the last thing I need. What I do want is prayer and compassion for my children and me. What I want for others is for someone to believe them and possibly approach them about what is going on behind their closed doors if signs are pointing to domestic violence. My home appeared to be a safe, healthy, Christian home. It took awhile before I was able to admit to myself that I was a "battered woman". Chances are, you know a "battered woman". What are you going to do to help? The first step is to educate yourself on this topic. Do not allow yourself to think my situation is rare. I am telling you-IT IS NOT! It is far too common. Some secular studies show at least 1 in 5 women are in an abusive relationship. Other independent studies are showing 40% to 50% of families are affected first hand by domestic violence at least two times yearly.

Making the Escape

The most dangerous time for a victim is when she/he is leaving or ending the relationship with the abuser. This would be why a victim may be more fearful of leaving rather than staying. Most victims don't want to leave. They just want the abuse to stop. It is not an easy decision to make. I went back and forth for two years trying to decide whether to stay or leave. When I understood that it was really "abuse" going on in our home, the questions became when and how do I leave. Ladies, be careful. Safety Planning is critical. Here are some things to consider:

- Know where your local domestic violence shelters are located
- Have a bag packed and waiting with clothes, snacks and drinks and other necessities for you and your children.
- Take your children with you.
- Have Pepper Spray or something similar
- Tell a trusted friend or family member
- Give NO signs to him you are leaving. (Do NOT threaten to leave)
- Have shot records, birth certificates, medications, social security cards, and any financial information in a safe place.
- Get a Post Office Box.

- Set aside some cash. When buying groceries it may be possible to write a check and get some cash weekly. Save birthday and Christmas money.
- Have a calling card.
- Get a cell phone to use when you leave. Make sure the cell phone bill will go to your Post Office Box so no one knows who you have called or where you have gone.
- Start a notebook with dates and a description of the abuse that occurred. Keep all evidence and "help" resources hidden.
- If you work and have direct deposit into a joint account, have your paycheck mailed to your Post Office Box.
- Take out an Emergency Protection Order. The piece of paper will not protect you, but makes it much easier for the justice system to protect you and your children. You will probably need your notebook for this. It helps if you can give the judge dates.
- Do not return to your home no matter what until you know it is safe.
- If you do not have time to prepare, but need to leave immediately, just go. Your life is much more important than a bag of clothes.

*Every situation is different. Therefore, safety planning will be a little different for everyone. Contact your local shelter for more information or counseling so you can make appropriate plans.

As I was in the process of leaving my husband, God was in control. Two weeks before I left, God spoke to me and I knew He released me to leave my home. My car had a hole in the brake-line and could not be driven. I did not know for sure when I was leaving until five days before. Steve accused me of losing his motorcycle keys in the most recent move two weeks earlier. He blew up. He pushed me around, and grabbed my wrist so hard I wondered if it was broken. Of course, many unkind words were mingled in there. Within an hour or so I tried to take a picture, but I could not hold the camera far enough away to get a clear picture. After a couple hours, I could move my wrist again and knew it was not broken. He was leaving for a youth retreat in three days and I decided at that point, it was the safest time to get out. I spent the next few nights crying and praying.

My father-in-law fixed my brake-line the day after Steve left for the retreat. It was so weird to know what I was going to do the next day as his parents were at our house. By this time, I had everything I needed to take with me in the bottom of the closet. The gun Steve had in his possession was in my car because the morning before, I removed it from his truck so he couldn't use it to hurt me or himself. God showed me in many ways He was with me. I wish I could say the church of God was with me. When I knew it was time to make an escape, I called a local church very close to my home. I gave them enough information to understand I needed their help, but not much more. I asked the lady if someone could come get my children's beds and just take them back to the church. Then I would send a Christian couple to come pick them up. No one would know who did what and I wouldn't ever tell.

She responded, "It is not the church's position to do that kind of thing. We will be praying for you and let us know if you need anything." My thoughts were, 'Well, then who's position is it? It's not like my church will help. My husband is a minister there. The shelter is hours away and they can't come that far. I had been so isolated, my closest friend was very far away and I didn't want her to be seen by my neighbors, which is why I needed the church to take the beds somewhere else. My kids love their beds and I wanted them to at least have the security of their own bed. I can do without a lot, but I have to take care of my babies. They are only one and three and never asked to be brought into this nightmare. Sure, pray for me. Sometimes God wants us to put hands and feet to our prayers.' I called a Christian I had not talked to in quite awhile and asked if she would help. She used those hands, feet and a van. That meant a lot to me. The shelter did not have baby beds, which concerned me before, but now it was a relief. God was with me and provided the help I needed.

The night I left, I had stress and peace. The two can co-exist at times. I put the boxes, snacks, drinks and blankets in the car. I put the kids in the car to go to a drive-in restaurant where my cell phone had service so they could tell Daddy good-night. I talked to Steve and reminded him that if we were at home, the phone would not have service. I told him I loved him. I did everything I could to show Steve love. When I left, the refrigerator and freezer were full of quick and pre-made meals. The house was cleaner than ever and I left a note written with love on the table. I wished so much it didn't have to be this way. I begged him to get counseling for the millionth time the night before he left for the retreat. Of course, he refused. While we were at the drive-in parking lot, my "Christian bed moving friends" were at my house taking care of business. When I pulled back on to the highway, I went to a car wash to vacuum the car. We were on our way to make sure the house was how I wanted it to be left. It was very dark and after driving about twenty minutes, we drove passed a hospital that was located about forty-five minutes from our house. I had turned the wrong way and was so tunnel-visioned that I didn't even notice. I turned around and started driving again. Forty-five minutes later, I placed the note I had prayed over on the end table. Isaac asked where we were going. I told him, "To a fun place. Sometimes we just have to go to other places for a while." "What to Say" should be a class offered in high school. As we got closer to the shelter, I called to say we were almost there. The lady on the other line said they were full. We couldn't come there. I asked if I could sit on their couch for a few minutes and wind down. She said, "No, we are full." My counselor from there had told me I could. That was my plan. If they were full, they would find a place for us to stay. Well, they didn't and I was doing everything I could to hold back the tears so my children wouldn't panic. We checked into a hotel around one o'clock a.m. and had to pay way too much for six hours. The girl working the desk called my room from her home and offered to bring us food. I thanked her and said we were fine. The next morning she said she knew what was wrong because she was once in my shoes and gave me ten dollars. She said she wished she could help more. Isaac asked me where we stayed and I called it "the place with the beds". He remembered that for months. That night was memorable. The kids and I shared a bed. They jumped, fought, kicked, tossed, and turned. I was glad when the sun came up. I went to the shelter and met with my counselor whom I had never met in person. She said she was so happy to see me. It was wonderful to hear that familiar, supportive voice that now had a face. She is a Christian and I have to believe she had been praying for me. She was the only one I could talk to in depth for the last several months. I called my mother-in-law so she would make sure someone would be there when Steve got home. He threatened suicide so many times; I didn't want him to be alone. She said okay. Then she called me back and said I was cruel for not telling him I was going to leave him. She was very unkind and acted like the whole thing was an exaggeration. She was clueless about how violent her son could be. At the shelter, I had some guidance about how to get an Emergency Protection Order. As I went towards the courthouse, I had a stop to make. I dropped the kids off at a park where the "bed-getter" watched them for me. Another friend (the one who caught the red flag) met me there to take the gun out of my car and take it to a safe place. She also gave me a cell phone so Steve couldn't see who I was calling. It was under a different name so the phone number could not even be traced back to me. At the courthouse, I went on a wild goose chase to find the right office for the EPO. The different offices kept telling me wrong. Finally in the right office, I was standing in line with my hand over my face sobbing. Keep in mind, I rarely cried. Two guys behind me were staring. Most likely because I was a mess. I was being forced to take legal action to protect myself and my children from my husband. It was disgusting. The judge looked at my application and immediately granted my request. He set a court date three weeks into the future where Steve would have the chance to speak. I picked up my children from the park where they were having a great time. We went back to the "fun place". They really were full, but they connected me with a different shelter about forty-five minutes away. I spoke with someone from the other shelter, which was a much smaller facility and was approved by phone to stay there. Back in the car we went. I picked up my survival kit from my friend on the way.

After we finally got to our new temporary home, it was about ten o'clock p.m. I remember checking in as my children ran wild. I tried to keep them still. My memory is cloudy about the details from that night. At the shelter, I met a friend named Amber. We had so much in common it was obviously a God thing. Six months later we still talk regularly and encourage each other. Her son and my children just love each other. After my dad met Amber, he told me we looked like sisters. We humored him too. I truly believe that when we really need a friend to understand, God will take care of that. If it is important to us, it is important to Him.

A couple weeks later, we went to court. I had little money and decided to represent myself rather than have an attorney. Steve had an attorney who made it look like I just went nuts and ran with the children. I had already decided before that day to only use the recordings if Steve said I was either lying or crazy. The attorney shot for both. After the judge heard what had gone on in our cozy little home, he was clearly very upset with my husband. As we listened to the six minutes of recordings, I cried and shook. It bothered me to hear it again, but I was more upset because I had to take such harsh measures to show the truth about my husband. The protection order was continued. The judge ordered full custody of our children along with child support to be placed in my hands. Although the courtroom scene was very stressful, the outcome could not have gone any better.

Life in a Shelter

As we were being checked into the shelter, Isaac and Renee were climbing up the walls in the office like little monkeys. I signed the paperwork and learned the rules. I got the grand tour of the place. Sarah (shelter staff) showed us the kitchen as I was feeling sick to my stomach at the thought of food. She gave me a bag of soap, shampoo and other things. She handed my two children a brown teddy bear for each of them and a sleeping bag type blanket with a matching pillow and bear that was made by some ladies at a church a few towns away. It was comforting to know that someone put that much effort into helping children feel more secure as they came to stay in a shelter. The love of Christ running through their veins is what drove them to make those blankets for children they would never meet on earth. They also put a Gospel tract with the bundle they made, hoping it would play a role in the child meeting Christ someday.

Well, speaking of blankets, we needed those blankets a few days later. Temperatures dropped into the 30's and 40's at night. If it were my house, the heat would have been turned on. But it wasn't. If it were light, I'm convinced we would have seen our breath. Yes, it was <u>that</u> cold. My children fell asleep. I couldn't. I checked on them all through the night and thought to myself, "What am I going to do?". The next day I was going to the store to see how much a small heater would cost. Staff informed me it was against fire code. Cost did not matter. One more teeth chattering night and I got a heater. For a few nights I turned the heater on in my new friend's room across the hall until she and her son fell asleep. Then I brought it in our room. In the mornings, she would wake me up at 5:30 so I could hide the heater. Crazy? No, just cold. But, at the same time I felt closer to my God than ever. He showed me where my strength comes from. When I am weak, I am strong.

Not everyone shared my faith in God. Sometimes the question came to mind, "Which are worse, the elements inside or the elements outside?" Women would come and go, while others stayed for weeks. Two women moved in one day. They were lovers and shared a room. They acted like lovers by the way they spoke to each other. My children and I did everything I could think of that day to keep them from seeing the same sex relationship they shared. They were nice, but I didn't want such impressionable minds to think it was normal. So we enjoyed the park, a restaurants play area, and the store. By the next day, the two women had left. I had tried to show them the love of Christ and spoke to them quite a bit while my children were sleeping. They seemed to be "shelter hoppers" and were proud of it. I was not too sad when they were told they had to leave. Two residents had moved on. Then we had two new members to our family. A mother and her 13 year old daughter joined us. The daughter was well behaved, talented, and very pleasant to be around. Her mother's biggest talent was fitting the four letter f-word into every sentence. Her mother was loud and verbally abusive to her daughter. It was so sad. Her awful language was used with her daughter. I was waiting for one of my children to repeat it. They never did. Her roughness did frighten them. I know she only acted like that because she was hurt, but it frightened me a little too. One day she started asking me questions. When I spoke to her about Jesus and how He had been by my side, she basically said He had also been by her f***ing side and blessed her so much. She definitely had some type of Christian influence in her life. She had some knowledge of the scripture. She was nice and open minded when we sat in our living room together. There was still an undercurrent of a rough lifestyle though. As the different women came and went, I was hoping to be able to leave the shelter soon. Sometimes it was peaceful and other times it was not quite as much of a healing place.

Some people were really upset about the rules. I understand there must be order and rules. Of course it was not enjoyable, but I knew the alternative. The alternative had brought us to the "fun place". Here are some rules I am talking about: 7am wake-up time, 9pm curfew, mandatory meetings, chores, children must stay very close to parent 24/7 which made even showering a real challenge. All phone calls we made were documented. My son's temperature kept spiking one night. I had to ask for my fever reducer and the shelter's thermometer all through the night. All medicines stay locked up. Here are some other issues:

- Much of the food was expired. My macaroni and cheese was a funny shade of brown. After we ate it, I noticed it expired two years ago. I'm still grossed out! I started buying my own groceries. Everything a resident purchased had to be properly labeled.
- The phone rang all through the night.
- One bathroom was shared. My children were too small to shower and had to sit in the tub. I scrubbed it, but it just didn't seem clean enough.
- We shared a community washer and dryer. Clothes came up missing. I lost 20 pounds in 3 weeks so it wasn't like my clothes fit anyway. At least I was skinny again. Stress at least helped me with that.
- We had to check in and out before going anywhere.
- Some family members found joy in the knowledge I was in a shelter. Misery loves company.

- Some Christians showed love and some showed the cold shoulder.
- I did not have a coat and it was nearly winter.
- The bed was not "my" bed.
- There was a security camera in the living room
- No privacy.
- We shared the television in the only living room. I had little control over what my children watched.

The list could go on.

After leaving the shelter...

I didn't have a screwdriver and my car needed a new headlight.

I used glue to wrap Christmas presents because I forgot Scotch tape doesn't exist in my new home.

Natural gas costs were rising.

I need small nails to hang my only clock.

Don't laugh at my new home. We really do live here. There just isn't a lot of furniture yet.

Those people at the church were so kind to help with staple type food, but how can I open it with out a can opener?

Did you know you can no longer buy a toilet brush at the store where everything is a dollar?

As my parents gave my children fruit snacks one day, my oldest said, "Mommy said this kind is too expensive." I'm just trying to be careful with my resources.

Did you know there is a hook up fee to have all utilities turned on?

I'm still skinny! And my clothes are still too big!

We ate with disposable plasticware (reused it too) for 3 weeks, but my own home sure beats a shelter.

Four women left the shelter around the same time. Four months later, none of the four had a bed. I guess it isn't a huge priority because our resources are going to other areas.

Notes from my journal from the first week in shelter

Everyone is saying the group here is a really good group. One of the best groups of residents the shelter has had. There are no drug addicts, alcoholics…just a group of very "normal" women. Many residents and staff are Christians. (I described the other 3 residents) the shelter isn't bad. At the same time, I don't want to stay here for long. It's clean, safe, and we laugh a lot. Everyone picks up after themselves. It is hard to keep two small children by my side at all times, but they are being very good. They are sleeping better here than at home. Isaac takes naps without any trouble at all. He isn't coming out of the room to say, "Daddy slams doors when he gets mad", "Daddy talks mean to you", or "Daddy scares me when he talks loud." He did that at home every day during nap time. He isn't making that nervous snorting noise much at all. Renee is just a giggle box. For a few days now, before she gets out of the highchair after eating, she says "snack". She wants to eat again before I have time to wash her off. There are 20 steps here that lead to our room. She has learned the words step, horse, and apple. My acne is clearing up because of less stress. Imagine that! We cook our own meals, do our own laundry, have daily chores… For the last 3 nights, it has been freezing in our rooms (30's and 40's outside) and no heat other than my little secret heater. Today we got a heater in the hallway. I hope it helps tonight. It's bound to be at least a little better. A crisis line is here so when the phone rings, it sounds like a school bell. Then we know someone else needs help. The doorbell is loud. If you go outside, the door will lock behind you. There are many security cameras. During the day it is usually just me, Isaac, and Renee here. Some are at work, and some are visiting family. There is some (very little) privacy, but it just isn't "home". Isaac asked to go home for the first time this morning. I told him we will soon. I am a little nervous about leaving. Steve told me today that he would never hurt me. He also said, "Do you realize you haven't talked to me since Thursday?" He doesn't want to give me any space. I'm in this shelter because I'm afraid of him and for good reason. I hope everything goes okay when I leave here. I told Sarah tonight that I wasn't sure what to do with the EPO. She said if he loves me he should respect me and shouldn't care so much that I keep the EPO. It concerns me to drop it because he wants it dropped so badly. I'm going to talk to (the marriage counselor at a specific church) about this.

I met some interesting, strong, and courageous abused women. Some women returned to their abusive homes. I wondered as they left if their picture, along with the funeral arrangements, would be on the news someday. It is amazing how close people can get when they share a home together. I think about them sometimes and wonder how they are doing. There is no way to find out.

Identifying an Abusive Relationship

The following lists and references from other resources are to give specific examples of abuse. This should make it a little easier to identify an abusive relationship.

TYPES OF ABUSE

Abusive Behavior Checklist

Yes or No

_____I feel that my partner is trying to run my life.

_____I feel that my opinion or emotions don't matter in our relationship.

_____My partner cuts me down and calls me names.

_____My partner 'forbids' me to do things like see a friend, wear a certain thing, or do something I want to do.

_____I find myself asking my partner's permission to spend time alone with friends or to engage in activities that don't include him or her.

_____I am often accused of flirting when I talk to friends of the opposite sex; my partner is very suspicious and jealous of me.

_____I try to please my partner, only to be criticized again and again.

_____When we argue, my partner always has to 'win' the argument, and won't really listen to my side of the story.

_____I am sometimes afraid of my partner.

_____I feel nervous or afraid to refuse my partner's sexual advances.

_____I have been threatened by my partner (with a break-up, with physical harm, with suicide, etc.).

_____My partner has destroyed or stolen my property to punish me.

_____My partner has hit, kicked, slapped, pushed, or otherwise struck me during an argument.

What is Emotional Abuse?

_____My partner blames me or anything that goes wrong in our lives.

_____My feeling are ridiculed by my partner.

_____My partner never accepts responsibility for his own actions.

_____Everything I say or do is criticized by my partner.

_____My partner tells me other people don't really like me.

_____I can't clean the house in a way that suits my partner.

_____My partner wants meals on the table at certain times, but what I cook is criticized.

_____My partner says I don't drive the car well.

_____My partner makes fun of me in front of family and friends.

_____My partner says I'm crazy.

_____My partner says or does things, then denies it.

_____My partner accuses me of wanting to be with other men.

_____My partners tells me if I leave him, I will never see the children again.

_____Although my children are the most important things in the world to me, my partner tells me I'm a bad parent and they would be better off without me.

_____My partner tells me that if I leave him, he will hurt my children, or my parents.

_____The family pet has been hurt by my partner and says he can do the same to me and the children.

_____I used to go to church every week, but my partner won't allow me to go anymore.

_____The children feel that we need to walk on eggshells around my partner, because we never know what will cause a temper outburst.

What is Physical Abuse?

_____My partner has slapped me.

_____My partner has pushed me.

_____My partner has thrown me across the room.

_____My partner has grabbed me by the arms or wrists.

_____My partner has kicked me.

_____My partner has thrown an object at me.

_____My partner has physically forced me to go from one place to another.

_____My partner has had his hands around my throat.

_____My partner has held me down on the floor or bed.

_____My partner has burned me with a cigarette on purpose.

_____My partner has pulled my hair.

_____My partner has punched me with his fist.

_____My partner has held a weapon pointed at me.

_____My partner has made threats to kills or hurt me.

_____My partner has hurt me with a weapon.

_____ My partner has caused me to have a black eye or bruise.

What is Verbal Abuse?

_____My partner tells me no one else would want me. I'm lucky she or he puts up with me.

_____My partner makes "jokes' about me that hurt and embarrass me.

_____My partner calls me names.

_____My partner says I can't cook, don't make enough money, don't clean right, am a bad parent, etc.

_____When I am upset about something, my partner refuses to discuss it.

_____My partner says hurtful things about me in front of other people.

_____My partner gives me the silent treatment.

_____My partner contradicts me about everything I say.

_____My partner says all our fights are my fault because I'm too sensitive.

_____My partner says that I make him or her angry by doing or saying things he or she has told me not to.

_____When I complain about something my partner has done, he or she often denies doing it.

What is Economic Abuse?

_____I want to work, but he won't allow it.

_____I have a job, but he demands that I hand my paycheck over to him.

_____He hides money from me.

_____I hide money from him so he won't get mad if I buy something.

_____The house is in his name only.

_____The checking and savings accounts are in his name only.

_____If I don't spend any money, I think we will get along better.

_____I must go to him for everything, even the money to buy feminine products.

_____He pays the credit card bills, but won't give me any cash.

_____I don't know how much money he earns or has in the bank.

_____I can't spend any money without being questioned by him.

_____He talked me into giving him power of attorney so he can sign .

What is sexual abuse?

_____I have no control over when we have sex; he makes the decisions.

_____I have no control over what kinds of sex we have; he does what he wants even if I'm saying no.

_____ He has a schedule of when he expects sex from me and I'm not allowed to say I don't want it.

_____He accuses me of flirting with or trying to seduce almost every male we come into contact with. He gets angry and won't believe my denials.

_____I'm not allowed to use birth control.

_____He has said he knows he is not the father of one or more of our children, although that is not true.

_____He has offered me to his friends sexually or threatens to.

_____He doesn't care when I say he is hurting me during sex.

_____He tells me he has sex with other women, but won't wear a condom with them or with me so that I am exposed to sexually transmitted diseases.

_____He controls what I wear – I have to be all covered up before I can go out.

_____He controls what I wear – he wants me to wear short tight clothes that make me look sexy.

_____He talks about my sexual behavior to his friends.

_____He talks about my sexual behavior to my children.

_____He threatens to find another woman to give him what he wants if I won't.

_____He starts having sex with me when I'm asleep.

Assessing Danger in Abusive Relationships

Although it is hard to predict which abusive men will eventually seriously injure or kill their victims, "yes" answers to the questions below are warning signs. Each additional "yes" means increased danger.

_____Have the assaults become more violent, brutal, and dangerous?

_____Has the perpetrator ever choked the victim? (Choking is regarded as a sign of danger because it is the most life-threatening action a batterer can do short of using a weapon.)

_____Has the perpetrator hurt or killed the family pets?

_____Are there knives, guns, or other weapons at home?

_____Does the perpetrator abuse alcohol or drugs such as speed, crack, cocaine, or heroin?

_____Does the perpetrator assault the victim while he is intoxicated or high?

_____Has the perpetrator threatened to kill the victim?

_____Does the victim believe that the perpetrator may seriously injure or kill her or himself?

_____Is the perpetrator assaultive during sex?

_____Is the perpetrator preoccupied with the victim?

_____Does the perpetrator follow the victim, monitor her whereabouts, and/or stalk her?

_____Is the perpetrator jealous, and does he imagine the victim is having affairs with other people?

_____Has the perpetrator threatened or tried to commit suicide?

_____Is the victim suicidal?

_____Is the perpetrator depressed or paranoid?

_____Has the perpetrator experienced recent deaths or losses?

_____Does the perpetrator have a history of assaulting other people or breaking the law?

_____Was the perpetrator beaten as a child, or did the perpetrator witness his mother being beaten?

_____Has the victim separated from the perpetrator, or is she considering separation?

_____Is the perpetrator making serious threats to kill the victim?

Most people know that a major barrier to getting help for people addicted to drugs or alcohol is persuading them to admit that they have a problem. We say that they are in denial, because they deny that they drink too much or have a drug problem. They don't want to admit the problem and have to face it, and maybe have to do something about it.

Similarly, women in battering relationships also tell themselves that "it isn't so bad", or "his family acts like that". They are in denial that they are in a abusive relationship. Their first step toward getting help will have to be admitting that their relationship is abusive.

The following is a checklist of behaviors that are present in relationships that are abusive:

Does your partner call you names?

Does he threaten you to make you do what he wants?

Has he threatened to hurt the children?

Has he ever threatened to kill himself or to kill you?

Does he time your trips to the store, or how long it takes you to get home from work?

Does he keep money from you?

Does he try to convince you that he is the only one that loves you?

Does he act one way in public and another way at home?

These are forms of power and control and begin the foundation of economic and emotional dependence on him.

Has he ever hurt your pets?

Has he ever destroyed property in order to threaten you?

Does he keep you from talking with or seeing family members or friends, or keep you from going to work or school?

Is he jealous of people you know or spend time with?

These behaviors begin to show the escalation of emotional abuse to physical abuse. The woman is in increasing danger in this relationship.

Has he ever hit you with something or thrown something at you?

Has he ever punched or kicked you?

Has he ever choked you?
Does he have a weapon? What is it?
Has he ever used it? Threatened to?
Has he ever forced you to have sex?

These are examples of physically abusive behaviors. The woman is in more serious danger with each battering incident.

How often does he do any of these things?
Have you ever gone to the hospital because of injuries
*   from an incident?*
Has he done any of these things to the children?
Are you blamed for his acts of violence?
Have you ever called the police? What happened?
Has he ever made threats to keep you from calling the
*   police?*

These questions help paint the picture of an abusive relationship. If you responded yes to ANY of the questions on this page, you need to think about whether your relationship is an abusive one.

The following is adapted from the "Power and Control Wheel" Duluth Domestic Abuse Intervention Project as found in Broken Children, Grown-up Pain by Paul Hegstrom.

Emotional Abuse

Put-downs. Name-calling. Mind games. Mental coercion. Extreme controlling behaviors. Conditional affection. Loss of identity.

Threats

Threats to end relationship. Threats to do harm emotionally or physically. Threats to life, to take the children, to commit suicide, or to report to the authorities. Forcing abused to break the law.

Economic Abuse

Restrictions on employment. Making the abused ask for money. Giving the abused an allowance and taking any money the abused earns. Requirement to account for every penny spent while grocery shopping.

Intimidation

Use of looks, actions, gestures, loud voice, or cursing to generate fear. Continual arguing. Abused to say what abuser wants to hear.

Property Violence

Punching walls, smashing things, and destroying property. Breaking down doors, pounding tables, abuse of pets, and so on.

Silence

Use of silence as a weapon. Cannot or will not communicate. Often lacks the mechanism to express emotions.

Isolation

Controls what is done, who is seen, who is talked to. Limits or listens in on phone calls. Sabotages car. Restriction of outside interests. Frequent moves. Required to stay in house. Restricts access to mail. Deprived of friends.

Use of Children

Use of children to give messages. Use of visitation rights as a way to harass. Use of child support as leverage.

Humiliation

Hostile humor. Public humiliation. Criticism. Denigrating appearance, parenting skills, housekeeping skills, cooking, and so on. Required to eat foods that abused does not like.

Responsibility Abuse

Making abused responsible for everything in life (bills, parenting, and so on).

Spiritual Abuse

Use of scripture and words like "submission" and "obey" to abuse. Spiritual language.

Sexual Abuse

Demanding unwanted or bizarre sexual acts. Physical attacks to sexual parts of the body. Treatment of the abused as a sex object. Interruption of sleep for sex. Forced sex. Extreme jealousy.

Use of Male Privilege

Treatment of the abused like a servant. Unilateral decision-making. Acting like "master of the castle".

Physical Abuse

Beating. Biting. Choking. Grabbing. Hitting. Kicking. Pinching. Pulling hair. Punching. Pushing. Restraining. Scratching. Shaking. Shoving. Slapping. Excessive tickling. Twisting arms. Using weapons. Spanking. Smothering. Tripping.

Power

Denial of basic rights. Using legal means of forcing power. Deprivation of private or personal life. Mandated duties. Controlling the amount of bath water used.

Stalking

Spying. Following to activities (store, church, work, and so on). Extreme distrust and jealousy.

Four Critical Characteristics of an Abusive Argument:

From the book <u>Why does he do that?</u> By Lundy Bancroft.

You may find that each disagreement with your partner is unique and can start in any of a thousand ways, yet it can only arrive at four or five different endings-all of them bad. Your gnawing sensation of futility and inevitably is actually coming from the abusive man's thinking about verbal conflict. His outlook makes it impossible for an argument to proceed toward anything other than the fulfillment of his wishes—or toward nowhere at all.

Four features stand out:

1. The abuser sees an argument as war.

His goal in a verbal conflict is not to negotiate different desires, understand each other's experiences, or think of mutually beneficial solutions. He wants only to *win*. Winning is measured by who talks the most, who makes the most devastating or "humorous" insults (none of which is funny to his partner), and who controls the final decision that comes out of the debate. He won't settle for anything other than victory. If he feels he has lost the argument, he may respond by making a tactical retreat and gathering his forces to strike again later.

Under this layer, there is an even deeper stratum in many abusive men where we unearth his attitude that *the whole relationship is a war*. To this mind-set, relationships are dichotomous, and you're on either one end or the other: the dominator or the submitter, the champ or the chump, the cool man or the loser. He can imagine no other way.

2. She is always wrong in his eyes.

It is frustrating, and ultimately pointless, to argue with someone who is certain beyond the shadow of a doubt that his perspective is accurate and complete and that yours is wrong and stupid. Where can the conversation possibly go?

The question isn't whether he argues forcefully or not. Many non-abusive people express their opinions with tremendous conviction and emotion yet still allow themselves to be influenced by the other person's point of view. On the other hand, it isn't hard to tell when someone is refusing to grapple in good faith with your ideas and instead is just reaching for whatever stick he thinks will deal the heaviest blow to your side. When your partner says to you disparagingly, "Oh, the real reason why you complain about how I argue is that you can't deal with my having strong opinions," he's diverting attention from the tactics he uses. He is also reversing reality, which is that *he* can't accept *your* differences of opinion and doesn't want to let his thinking be influenced by yours. (And on the rare occasions when he does adopt your ideas, he may claim they were his to begin with.)

3. He has an array of control tactics in conflicts.

My clients have so many ways to bully their way through arguments that I couldn't possibly name them all, but the abuser's most common tactics are listed in the box below:

Sarcasm

Ridicule

Distorting what you say

Distorting what happened in an earlier interaction

Sulking

Accusing you of what he does,
or thinking the way he thinks

Using a tone of absolute certainty and
final authority—"defining reality"

Interrupting

Not listening, refusing to respond

Laughing out loud at your opinion or perspective

Turning your grievances around to use against you

Changing the subject to *his* grievances

Criticism that is harsh, undeserved, or frequent

Provoking guilt

Playing the victim

Smirking, rolling his eyes, contemptuous facial expressions

Yelling, out shouting

Swearing

Name-calling, insults, put-downs

Walking out

Towering over you

Walking toward you in an intimidating way

Blocking a doorway

Other forms of physical intimidation,
such as getting too close while he's angry

Threatening to leave you

Threatening to harm you

Conversational control tactics are aggravating no matter who uses them, but they are especially coercive and upsetting when used by an abusive man because of the surrounding context of emotional or physical intimidation. I have rarely met an abuser who didn't use a wide array of the above tactics in conflicts; if you consider an argument with a partner to be a war, why not use every weapon you can think of? The underlying mind-set makes the behaviors almost inevitable.

The abusive man wants particularly to *discredit* your perspective, especially your grievances. He may tell you, for example, that the "real" reasons why you complain about the way he treats you are:

- You don't want him to feel good about himself.
- You can't handle it if he has an opinion that differs from yours, if he is angry, or if he is right.
- You are too sensitive, you read too much into things, or you take things the wrong way.
- You were abused as a child or by a former partner, so you think everything is abuse.

These are all strategies he uses to avoid having to think seriously about your grievances, because then he might be obligated to change his behaviors or attitudes.

The abusive man's goal in a heated argument is in essence to get you to *stop thinking for yourself* and to *silence you*, because to him your opinions and complaints are obstacles to the imposition of his will as well as an affront to his sense of entitlement. If you watch closely, you will begin to notice how many of his controlling behaviors are aimed ultimately at discrediting and silencing you.

4. He makes sure to get his way-by one means or another.

The bottom line with an abuser in an argument is that he wants what he wants-today, tomorrow, and always-and he feels he has a right to it.

Phrases from an abuser

I own you/You are so controlling/You do what I want you to do/Can't you do anything right?/You don't deserve to live/ You sexless lump of person/You're frigid/You piece of sh**/ Shut up before I kill you/Be submissive/You better be f***ing submissive before I f***ing kill you/I hate you/You say some of the stupidest things to people. No wonder nobody likes you/You can't cook/All you cook is little sh** meals/I want a real wife/Oh, you're so abused. Why don't you go to one of those shelters? /If you don't like how I treat you, leave. But I'm keeping the kids/You're an unfit mother/I'm taking the kids. Eventually they will forget you/I know you have another man/I know you're getting it (sex) somewhere/Do you do **anything** during the day?/No, I won't watch the kids. You had all day to take a shower/You don't know anything about the Bible. You need to be submissive and get in your place/I don't care how loud I snore. If you sleep on that couch, your stuff will be on the curb tomorrow/Other women can handle it. Why can't you? /You are just as dumb as your idiot parents/ I'll bust your teeth out of your head/ Maybe God will just knock you off/I pray our children will get their intelligence from me. I thought that before I married you/Since you got a job, you think you wear the pants in the family/You screw up everything you touch/ You do everything half-a**/Bullsh**. All you ever have to say is bullsh**/You have no ambition/You couldn't get a master's degree if you tried/My mother kept a clean house. Why can't you? /You mother f*****/You're lucky I let you live/Lesbian/ You're a human snafu (when I asked what that was supposed to mean, he said it is a human f*** up)/Do you have a brain in there?(as he poked at my head)/I'll chop you up into tiny pieces and spread you all over…

The things a person says to hurt another person can really be destructive sometimes. I debated on whether or not to include this part. Typing foul language near scripture was somewhat uncomfortable. At the same time, if we want to play a role in stopping domestic violence, we must not candy coat it. I believe it is important to "hear the man in action". My husband said these things to me, but these words are typical coming out of an abuser's mouth. If you are hearing these types of phrases from your husband, you are not in a healthy relationship. You are not the one with the problem. He is completely out of control.

A Crash Course in "Red-Flags"

Sometimes, seeing the "red flags" can be difficult. It will be especially difficult to identify for yourself. There are a few reasons why. Domestic Violence is typically cyclical. There are 3 stages the abuser goes through. The first is the tension building stage. This includes, of course, escalating tension and anger, arguing, blaming, criticizing, and minor incidents. During this time the victim is "walking on eggshells" and trying to keep peace. She can usually sense the storm is on its way. The second stage is when the violence explodes. The abuser looses control and is highly abusive; physically, verbally, emotionally and/or sexually. The victim feels trapped and is traumatized. The last stage is the honeymoon period or the calm stage. The abuser may deny what happened, apologize, promise to change, manipulate, or give gifts. The victim is confused and may think this isn't abuse because he isn't in a rage all of the time. He has a good side. She may feel responsible for the incident.

The abuser has the Jekyll and Hyde personality. His mood can swing without warning. Often, he is like two different people depending on who is around. The psalmist understands this man's character.

Psalms

55:20

My companion attacks his friends; he violates his covenant

55:21

His speech is smooth as butter, yet war is in his heart; his words are more soothing than oil, yet they are drawn swords.

Proverbs also has some words of wisdom to share about dealing with this man.

Proverbs

26:23

Like a coating of glaze over earthenware are fervent lips with an evil heart.

26:24

A malicious man disguises himself with his lips, but in his heart he harbors deceit.

26:25

Though his speech is charming, do not believe him, for seven abominations fill his heart.

26:26

His malice may be concealed by deception, but his wickedness will be exposed in the assembly.

26:27

If a man digs a pit, he will fall into it; if a man rolls a stone, it will roll back on him.

26:28
A lying tongue hates those it hurts, and a flattering mouth works ruin.

He may only show his violent side in his own home with his family. This makes it more difficult for his family to get help. The victim might feel as though no one will believe her. She might be right. If someone approaches you and says something is wrong, believe the victim until you can prove otherwise. You don't know what happens in her home. The abuser might be a factory worker, police officer, minister, judge, teacher, or deacon. Domestic violence affects women of all races, ages, education levels, economic status and religions. My husband happens to be a youth minister with training in counseling and ministry. People told me frequently how wonderful he was. One Sunday morning a deacon approached me and said my husband was "a gentle giant". I wanted to cry, but instead nodded.

All people and all situations are different. Not all abusers or victims will show the classic signs. We may not see the signs because the abusive side of the relationship is kept secret.

An abuser may:
- Have witnessed abuse as a child or been abused.
- Have a severe temper. (This is usually masked in public.)
- Have distorted sense of entitlement.
- Be unstable.
- Be negative.
- Hate authority.
- Demand respect.
- Promise to stop being violent.
- Have a very strong opinion of a "woman's role" and "man's role".
- Have a drug or alcohol problem.
- Have a mental illness.
- Have low self esteem but cover it.

- Seem extremely religious or self-righteous.
- Be condemning.
- Be critical.
- Be kind and gentle most of the time, but is violent when the mood swings.
- Blames others for all problems.
- Be deceitful.
- Have narsistic characteristics. (How does everything affect me and are my needs being met?)
- Refuse counseling.
- Take on the role as parent and "punish". "You act like a child so I'll treat you like one."
- Appear to have it all together.
- Expect too much from his wife and children.
- Isolate the victim.
- Have no accountability.
- Take the scriptures out of context to meet their needs.
- May use the word "submit" in a way that God never intended it to be used.
- Be jealous or possessive.
- Relocate frequently.
- Church hop.
- Job hop.
- Say how awful abusive men are.
- Be suicidal.
- Be depressed.
- Seem overly humble or very prideful.
- Be very emotionally dependent on his partner.
- Be possessive.

The victim may display signs such as:
- Fear of the violent partner
- Embarrassed of situation
- May not see or spend time with friends or family because of their partner's jealousy

- Always agree with partner to avoid a fight
- Frequently apologizes for their partner's behavior
- Fear of partner's temper
- Have been forced, pushed, or manipulated into having sex when ill, tired, in pain, or just not feeling up to it
- Be forced to miss or leave work
- Not allowed to leave the house regardless of the reasons
- Feels the need to justify where she goes and who she sees
- Receives frequent "check-in" phone calls
- Must "check-in" too often
- Nervousness
- View situation as normal at times, but knows it is not
- Gets injuries and blames it on being clumsy
- Lack of energy
- A healthy breast feeding mother may stop producing milk due to stress.
- May be obsessed with things to subconsciously distract herself (budgeting, shopping, appearance, cleaning, books)
- Monthly cycle becomes irregular due to stress
- Frequent backache (Severe back pain is not uncommon among abused women.)
- Frequent headache
- Frequent illness (real or perceived)
- Bruises or cuts
- Racing pulse
- Nightmares or sleeplessness
- Jumpy
- Self destructive
- Depression
- Drug or alcohol addiction
- Crying, but won't say why
- Defend partner

- Anxiety attacks
- Uncomfortable around men
- Stomach problems
- Body aches

*Doctors and dentists (if victim can go) have a unique opportunity to notice and make note of injuries to the mouth or reoccurring illnesses. If you work in this field, please be prepared to offer resources if you even suspect a problem. You might be saving a life. You can always offer a brochure to her and say something like, "I'm trying to make more women aware of what an unhealthy relationship looks like and ways to get out. If you know a woman in a situation, please pass this on to her."

*Identify Theft – Her identify has been stolen. Nearly all verbally abused women will slowly lose their spirit. As the abuser writes awful, destructive things on her heart, she will begin to believe his lies. Others don't have the right to "name" us. That right solely belongs to God. I recently heard a sermon on this topic. It really spoke to me. When you see women's spirits fading, something is seriously wrong.

If someone seems to be acting in unusual ways, there might be a really good reason. Be sensitive. When my family would go to church, my husband would attend the service. I was not allowed to leave our children with anyone. My husband would say a woman's job is to take care of her children. He wouldn't allow me to leave the children in the church nursery and he wouldn't allow me to bring our two toddlers in the sanctuary until I cried and begged to attend church. When the children made a noise in church, he often became angry with me or was harsh with them. The women in the nursery wondered why I always stayed in the nursery. They made comments such as, "You need to be in church", "We can take care of them", "It's only an hour", "You're being over protective", "Every mom needs a break." I appeared to be untrusting, unsociable and overbearing, but yet I wanted to go to church so badly. The children would have been fine with them and would have developed necessary social skills with Mom not around for an hour. The same women asked me to scrapbook with them. I wanted to scrapbook and build friendships, but my husband always had a reason for saying no. I told the women I had my pictures in a box ready to be creative and how excited I was. Then I had to make up excuse after excuse not to go. I was isolated even in my church. I so desperately wanted to say, "It's not me, it's him". After leaving my husband, I did not and have not received much support from that church. After some acknowledged there was a problem, they were then convinced that he is a safe person now. They are still seeing a different side of him than what he is showing me. I have been told I'm in sin for not reconciling with him. He must become healthy before I can start working on marriage issues with him. I want reconciliation, but true reconciliation does not just mean living together again.

Supporting a Friend

If you know someone who is being treated in a way that is inappropriate, support them as much as possible. Many victims don't have a "best friend" because they have been isolated. This person might be a co-worker, bank clerk, neighbor, friend, or a visitor at your church. If she approaches you and tells you she is being abused, believe her. Keep in mind you must be careful that the abuser's wrath doesn't turn to you. Do not let him know you know. This is to protect both you and the victim. It takes a lot of courage to tell that first person. Reassurance is so important. You may want to say things such as:

You don't deserve_____. No one deserves that.

I'm sorry you have been going through this alone until now.
(Stress the importance of physical and emotional safety of her and her children.)

I'm proud of you for sharing this with me. I know it was a hard decision to make.

I can only imagine how difficult it must have been.
(Remind your friend that abuse is never the fault of the victim.)

I'm worried about you.

You are a capable, intelligent, loveable, hardworking, talented beautiful person. (Maybe not in one sentence!)

You are wonderful mother.

I'm praying for you. (Pray for her and add hands and feet to those prayers where applicable.)

Give her a hug if you are a female. (The thought of being touched by a man may make her shutter.)

God never intended marriage to be like that.

You deserve love and respect.

(Help her find resources she may need.)

(Ask her if she knows what she is going to do without sounding like she should have an answer.)

What can I do to help?

You can trust me.

Keep everything she says completely confidential. If her abuser finds out she has told anyone, the consequence may be unimaginable. If you believe you need to call the police to report what you have been told, speak with a domestic violence educated professional first. That may or may not be an appropriate step. Have a code word that says, "Call the police" or, "He is in the room and I can't talk now."

Believe her no matter how unbelievable it may sound. Very few people lie about living in a violent home and many lie about living in a peaceful home. Whether she has bruises or other injuries at the time is often irrelevant. If she is injured, help her get medical attention. From the outside, you might have seen red flags, or a charming man that was a wonderful, sincere Christian person. Remember the Jekyll and Hyde thing. Believe the unbelievable. An abuser may appear to be very "anti-abuse". He could be clean cut or scrubby, handsome or unattractive, a judge or a factory worker, a minister or a bouncer, a doctor or construction worker, or large or small in build. Get the point? You don't live with him and it might seem really unbelievable to you.

-Let your words and actions show her you believe her and you care.

-Be patient. It may take awhile for the victim to decide to get out of the relationship. Stay supportive.

Do not minimize her experience. Chances are she isn't telling a fraction of what has happened. She has probably been sexually abused in one form or another, but you will never know what. Here are some suggestions of things that you shouldn't say.

- "I don't believe you." or anything that means it
- Every couple has arguments.
- Are you sure you two aren't just reacting to each other? (My mom helped with this one.)
- Have sex more often. (That will not stop the abuse.)
- Is there another man?
- You said he threatened to kill you, but it doesn't look like he did it.
- He helps people regularly and would give anyone the shirt off his back.
- He just has a hard time dealing with stress.
- You should have done _____ differently or better.
- He is a good provider.

- You can't support yourself.
- Leave him <u>now</u>. Are you crazy? (She must be ready to leave him or she will almost definitely not have the strength to stay separated until they both have received the help they need.)
- (Do not blame her in anyway.)
- You need to get over it.
- It's not like you are perfect either. It takes two to tango.
- Did he ever break a bone or punch you with a fist? (As if she should wait for that to happen.)
- As long as you plan to get back together/stay together, I will support you. (True reconciliation cannot take place with a violent person.)
- (If she doesn't want to tell her pastor, respect this. She may have a very good reason.)
- Do not twist the Bible to say a person is in sin because she wants herself and children to be safe.
- Do not suggest marriage counseling. Abuse is not a marriage issue. It is an individual issue that must be resolved before the marriage issue can be worked on. A very large majority of counselors including many Christian counselors are not equipped to deal with this type of situation. Marriage counseling sounds like the Christian thing to suggest, but it is not. It is like setting a match in front of a toddler. Abusers can often manipulate the counselor leading to more emotional injury to the victim. Many studies have showed marriage counseling does not stop domestic violence.

While I was waiting for the court date to arrive, Steve suggested we go to a Christian counselor. I called the counselor and he assured me he had experience in dealing with violent families and told me I could speak to him alone for the first few minutes of our appointment. I wanted someone to help our marriage. I agreed to marriage counseling also with the hope that he would act as a mediator to decide who will live in which of our houses. When I spoke to the counselor on the phone, he agreed to help with that. I told him I had recently left my husband due to his violent anger.

Our appointment began and I asked for a minute of one on one. I briefly explained the situation. I sensed he was minimizing what I was saying and told him I had months of documentation and some audio tape. My husband came back in and the counselor started trying to pinpoint when the problem began. Housing never came up, but the counselor did tell my husband in my presence that even if we have sex, it doesn't mean everything is okay. Was he suggesting that sleeping together soon was even an option? My husband had given me more than enough reason to believe he could and would actually end my life. So, having sex would be normal and should be mentioned nine days after fleeing my home? At the time, that comment bothered me, but it bothered me much more after I began to think more clearly. We ran out of time and scheduled an appointment for the next day.

At that appointment we discussed several things including dropping the Emergency Protection Order. This was also inappropriate. The counselor should not have discussed this with Steve present. I did not bring up the subject with him present. The counselor allowed my husband to manipulate me right in front of his face. We scheduled another appointment for about two weeks later.

During the EPO hearing, Steve's attorney used the fact that I agreed to go to marriage counseling against me. I stated that a mediator was needed to help determine where the children and I could live. I had already said I loved my husband and just wanted him to get help. I also asked the judge to allow us to be together with the exception of marriage counseling. The judge did make this exception, but the counselor had to be approved by the agency that taught the anger management classes Steve was court ordered to attend. The agency would not approve marriage counseling at that time. It was too soon. I cancelled the marriage counseling appointment for me, but Steve still had the option of going. He continued to see the same counselor. Around Christmas, Steve said the counselor suggested I had a boyfriend because I was not spending Christmas with my husband. I assured him again and again I was not cheating physically **or** emotionally. If that counselor really said that, he was very wrong. Steve also said he knew what went on in the few minutes I spoke to the counselor when he was not in the room. He said I told the counselor he physically abused me and that I had evidence like documentation and audio recordings. That is exactly what happened. I thought everything was supposed to be confidential. I guess it wasn't. I don't believe the counselor is a bad guy at all. He has probably helped many couples needing help over average marriage issues. Domestic violence just isn't his specialty. Now I understand a few of the reasons why a knowledgeable counselor should refuse to counsel a couple together in this type of situation. I have read many resources both Christian and secular that state very boldly that marriage counseling with both individuals present should be strongly advised against or refused. Once the abuse has been put to a stop, speaking to the couple together could be an option. I believe after a woman takes the huge step of leaving her husband, two things must happen before the relationship can begin to be restored. The abuse must stop completely. Then healing must take place. I might have just chased a rabbit, but it was an important rabbit to catch.

Why Does She Stay?

Looking at an abusive situation from the outside is much different that living it. From the outside, we might say something like, "RUN, RUN, RUN". That sounds easy enough. But there are many reasons why a woman may stay. A victim must work through these reasons in her own mind before she can leave with a healthy mindset. If someone pushes a victim to leave before she is ready, it is likely she will return to her abuser before either has received the help they need. The average battered woman will leave home seven times according to some statistics. I am convinced each time she returns, the violent episodes become more extreme. Sometimes, I wanted my phone counselor to tell me to leave. She never did. She said she supported me, but her place was not to tell me what to do. When she said she was very concerned about my safety, my brain was able to translate that into-it's probably time to get moving. Some reasons that entrap a woman or contribute to a woman returning to violence may not sound logical. Other reasons seem like very real issues. If an abused woman is concerned about an "irrational" reason, keep in mind that trauma can prevent anyone from thinking as clearly as they normally would. Imagine being terrorized and traumatized regularly. Remember too, she has more information regarding her situation than you have.

I do not believe it is totally necessary for a woman to leave her home in all cases of abuse. In many cases, I do believe leaving is the best thing. Sometimes she may need to leave temporarily. Other times it is probably best for the move to be permanent. A long time friend shared a little of her experience with me when she learned I had left my husband. Her one question was, "How far is too far?" When does the woman need to leave? At the time, I had no idea either. As time has progressed, I think I have an answer. All situations are different though, so don't take this as the Gospel. The Holy Spirit will have to guide her in making this decision. I believe that she needs to think seriously about leaving if

- he harms her or the children physically
- he threatens to harm her or the children physically
- she fears he is about to harm her or the children physically

If he is physically violent in any way one time, it will almost definitely happen again. If he is verbally abusive and she is being degraded by him, communication **may** be able to help the situation. If she is not in any fear for herself physically, it may be beneficial to approach him with how he makes her feel when he says____. Do **not** confront an abuser if he has ever been physically dangerous or made threats to harm physically. If the verbal abuse does not cease once she has approached him, it may be time to leave. "Sticks and stones may break my bones, but words will never hurt me." The person who said this years ago, must not have lived with a verbally abusive person. Words do hurt, and they can hurt for a really long time. No one deserves to be harmed in any way, especially in their own home.

I have a relative who stayed with her abusive husband for many years while I was growing up. I kept thoughts to myself such as, "is she stupid and why doesn't she just leave?" I am here to say she is not and was not stupid. She was probably thinking the same types of things that I thought as I remained with my husband.

Often, an abuser will make threats to keep her from leaving. He might make threats such as, "If you leave"…

I will kill you.

I will take the kids from you.

I will prove you are crazy.

I will harm/kill the children.

I will kill myself.

I cannot live without you.

The judge will see you are an unfit mother.

No one will believe your story that I abuse you, because I do not.

You will screw our kids up by breaking up our family.

You will go to hell. God hates divorce.

An abuser will tear his victim down to prevent her from leaving him. She will often start to believe things about herself, her abilities, or her rights that are false. Because of my lack of knowledge (and presents of brainwashing), I was actually fearful that God might judge me harshly if I left my husband due to his violence. After much prayer and looking in the Word of God for His wisdom, I began to see I had to leave. The Holy Spirit convicted me in a gentle way. I was enabling him to hurt our children and myself. Later, God clearly spoke to me in a dream which gave me confidence it was time to leave in the very near future. I left two weeks after the dream. During the times when I believed it was God's will that I got out, other thoughts would step in.

She may be thinking…

- How can I support us financially?
- Who can I turn to?
- I'm afraid of secular influence from the women's shelters.
- It's really not that bad.

- I feel sorry for him.
- Maybe he will get better.
- He does have a good side.
- I feel guilty.
- What if I miss him.
- Leaving and/or divorce is wrong.
- Who am I without him?
- He is their father. How can I take them away from him?
- Somehow I feel this is my fault.
- I should have _____.
- I don't think the police/courts can/will help.
- We just have marriage problems.
- If I leave, I have failed.
- What if he gets full custody?
- What if no one believes me?
- Where will we live?
- What if my church turns their back on me?
- What if he abducts our children?
    More than half of child abductions are the result of domestic violence.
- How do I stay safe after leaving?
- What if being without him is worse than being with him?

The "what ifs" could go on forever. They did for hours at night in my mind as I lied awake in bed and my husband snored loudly. The top two reasons on my list were these: What if he kills me? What if he abducts our children? I was also concerned about what kind of witness I would be when I left. Everyone thought we had the perfect Christian marriage. I didn't want to be a "stumbling block" by letting them in on my secret. My parents are not Christians and I thought if they find this out, it will give them a reason to believe Christians are hypocrites. Now I see the enemy put those thoughts in my head. God is plenty capable of taking care of Himself. My job is to obey Him. I don't need to protect Him by covering up the sins of my husband. Usually a combination of reasons will trap a woman in an unhealthy relationship. Some of the fears kept my children and me in a violent home and other fears motivated me to make preparations to get out safely and with very solid evidence. I really felt strongly that I had to "prove" my case. Audio taping an abuser can be very dangerous, but I was willing to take the risk. I do not recommend using a recorder. He came very close to catching me one night. That would have been bad!

Sometimes I wanted someone to hear us and call the police. He told me he would kill me if I called the police. He meant it. If someone else called and the cops busted the door down without warning, they would take him to jail. I would have time to get out safely. That was just wishful thinking. No one ever called the police for me. Surely, they could hear my screams and cries or his yelling, hitting things and throwing things. I know other women who escaped, but wished for the same type of intervention when they lived with their abuser.

As I have researched domestic violence in the last few months, law enforcement baffles me. Police officers from police departments all over the United States have actually admitted that when they get a domestic violence call, they wait a while before going to the scene. More than half of all injuries and deaths of law enforcement personnel are from these calls. The average abusive man in a rage will do most of his destruction in a matter of ten minutes or less. It is safer for the cop to wait until this time passes. If the victim had the courage or the physical ability to call for help, she wanted the police there before she even made the call. Wasted time could mean the end of her life.

Last week, in my local paper, I read a story about the police getting a call. They got there very quickly. They also forced entry! The man was taken to jail. The scene in this woman's house was so similar to a night I had experienced, but my husband hung up the phone so my night had no police. This woman got a chance to make that new beginning for her family with the help of the local police. I hope she took the opportunity. I read the article through tears. I can feel her pain. My local police department probably dreads those 911 calls also. They would have a good reason. I am so blessed to live in this city. They wouldn't make me defend myself for ten minutes. They don't hesitate. I have read about the cops that run from their fears. I believe they are out there. I have seen first-hand, the guys that do all they can to protect their community. I have also witnessed their kindness and compassion. If all police departments were like the one in my city, it would make a difference across the nation.

If you want to know why a victim did not call the police, she probably thought it was actually safer not to. Maybe it is true. Maybe it is not.

So why does she stay? Maybe she has been belittled for so long, she doesn't see that she has the right to live in a peaceful home.

What can the church do to help?

" Single mother" sounds, to many, as productive in society as a mosquito. In an abusive situation, the exact opposite is true. For a woman to leave the abuser is the most loving and courageous thing a mother can do for her child. When she leaves, she can create a healthy atmosphere for her child that she was unable to create before. She can teach her child by example. She is no longer being abused and the one learning by example can learn from a healthy parent. Women become better mothers when they are not being beat down verbally or physically. The child's chance of being abused or being an abuser when becoming an adult is significantly reduced when his/her mother puts a stop to the violence in her home. It may mean she needs a little financial help in the beginning to stop abuse before it starts in the next generation. Just help her. Do not give her time to ask. Many women end up on welfare until they can get their feet on the ground. I have been very blessed to be able to survive without a check from the government. God has blessed me with a very good job. I am very careful to manage my resources in a way to stretch it as far as it can be stretched. It isn't always easy. My God usually provides for us by using my paycheck. I definitely cannot count on child support. What about those who don't receive a pay check? Some women are not able to work immediately after leaving the breadwinner for their family. Health issues, mental state, fear, lack of education, lack of skill, pregnancy, or very small children may contribute to her inability to start working immediately. Welfare is not a bad choice for them temporarily. BUT, WHERE IS THE CHURCH? Where is the church? Where is the church? Before I get too carried away with where the church should be, I need to tell you something. When I moved to the shelter, I met Amber. She bragged on her church because of their actions. When she left the shelter a week before me, she called me with more good reports about this "Family of God". They listened to her concerns. They loved on her. They prayed for her. They kept her situation quiet. They supported her in her decisions. They befriended her. Although she attended church regularly before, her husband had built a wall in her old friendships. They took up a large collection of household supplies at church, but no one knew it was going to Amber. She was also given a large sum of cash in an envelope from a family. She still does not know which family it was. They chose to bless her without a "thank you" in return. I hope you see where I'm going with this. Her church exhibited Biblical action to the situation. They stood up like Jesus with skin on. I was so encouraged by these reports from her. God's people were acting like GOD'S PEOPLE!

Hebrews 6:10

God is not unjust; he will not forget your work and the love you have shown him as you have helped his people and continue to help them.

They will be rewarded for their obedience. They did not forget about their sister and their Father will not forget them.

When Jesus died on the cross, He died for the oppressed. He doesn't desire for us to be oppressed. When we are, it becomes the church's job to help.

Acts 10:38

how God anointed Jesus of Nazareth with the Holy Spirit and power, and how he went around doing good and healing all who were under the power of the devil, because God was with him.

Galatians 6:10

Therefore, as we have opportunity, let us do good to all people, especially to those who belong to the family of believers.

Acts 4:34-35

4:34

There were no needy persons among them. For from time to time those who owned lands or houses sold them, brought the money from the sales

4:35

and put it at the apostles' feet, and it was distributed to anyone as he had need.

Matthew 25:34-46

25:35

For I was hungry and you gave me something to eat, I was thirsty and you gave me something to drink, I was a stranger and you invited me in,

25:36

I needed clothes and you clothed me, I was sick and you looked after me, I was in prison and you came to visit me.'

25:37

"Then the righteous will answer him, 'Lord, when did we see you hungry and feed you, or thirsty and give you something to drink?

25:38

When did we see you a stranger and invite you in, or needing clothes and clothe you?

25:39

When did we see you sick or in prison and go to visit you?'

25:40

"The King will reply, 'I tell you the truth, whatever you did for one of the least of these brothers of mine, you did for me.'

25:41

"Then he will say to those on his left, 'Depart from me, you who are cursed, into the eternal fire prepared for the devil and his angels.

25:42

For I was hungry and you gave me nothing to eat, I was thirsty and you gave me nothing to drink,

25:43

I was a stranger and you did not invite me in, I needed clothes and you did not clothe me, I was sick and in prison and you did not look after me.'

25:44

"They also will answer, 'Lord, when did we see you hungry or thirsty or a stranger or needing clothes or sick or in prison, and did not help you?'

25:45

"He will reply, 'I tell you the truth, whatever you did not do for one of the least of these, you did not do for me.'

25:46

"Then they will go away to eternal punishment, but the righteous to eternal life."

James 1:27

Religion that God our Father accepts as pure and fault-less is this: to look after orphans and widows in their distress and to keep oneself from being polluted by the world.

James 2:13-18

2:13

because judgment without mercy will be shown to anyone who has not been merciful. Mercy triumphs over judgment!

2:14

What good is it, my brothers, if a man claims to have faith but has no deeds? Can such faith save him?

2:15

Suppose a brother or sister is without clothes and daily food.

2:16

If one of you says to him, "Go, I wish you well; keep warm and well fed," but does nothing about his physical needs, what good is it?

2:17

In the same way, faith by itself, if it is not accompanied by action, is dead.

2:18

But someone will say, "You have faith; I have deeds." Show me your faith without deeds, and I will show you my faith by what I do.

1 Corinthians 12:22-26

12:22

On the contrary, those parts of the body that seem to be weaker are indispensable,

12:23

and the parts that we think are less honorable we treat with special honor. And the parts that are unpresentable are treated with special modesty,

12:24

while our presentable parts need no special treatment. But God has combined the members of the body and has given greater honor to the parts that lacked it,

12:25

so that there should be no division in the body, but that its parts should have equal concern for each other.

12:26
If one part suffers, every part suffers with it; if one part is honored, every part rejoices with it.

When a woman is forced to begin again without the help of her husband, the church should help her as though she is a widow. Her children should also get "extra" love from their church family. When I say "church family", I don't mean the church that holds her membership. I am talking about anyone who has the Holy Spirit. You might be a neighbor, co-worker, or just an acquaintance. Don't expect "her church" to do God's work. The church really has a lot of responsibility. If people work together, each person has a small amount of responsibility. If everyone neglects the things they should do, you might see a sister in Christ return to the abuse or leave the church altogether. A woman should not have to ask for help once her church knows her situation. It can be humiliating for her. The church should be sensitive to her needs, help where they know she needs it, and gently ask her what they can do. The church should act as a crutch and help her to stand on her legs as time progresses. They should not help her and then drop her. A pastor specifically told me they would not drop me. When we moved into the shelter, I asked around about churches. I found one to attend for the next week or so until we were back in a familiar area. It was a church plant. The first week we attended, the people were very friendly and offered to take Isaac and Renee to the nursery. I declined and thanked them. During the meet and greet time, several people welcomed us. A man (a deacon) greeted the children and me. He told Isaac that he was going to break his leg or something crazy like that. Most three-year-old boys would laugh and come back with something boyish. Isaac cried and cried. Isaac had lived in a home where he heard threats, not jokes. I told the guy he was a little nervous around men. Then the service began. As my children got louder, I took them to the nursery and stayed with them. A very kind lady asked me about myself in the small room with toys and a few toddlers playing. I was vague with her, but gave her enough information to know I needed her to put me on her prayer list. When the invitation began, she said she would watch the children for me. I started to go towards the sanctuary. Isaac and Renee got hysterical. The lady (the deacon's wife) went with me to the sanctuary to help maintain my children while the pastor prayed for me. I quickly filled the pastor in on my prayer needs. He was very compassionate. The deacons and leadership were also loving and concerned. I was encouraged. Because my husband was a minister at my church, I couldn't return anytime soon. This new church was filling in the gap. They said, "If you need anything let us know" and gave me contact information. "We will not drop you", they promised. Well, I guess I fell between the cracks. The next week, we attended the church again. I gave the pastor's wife my name and cell phone number. I needed someone to talk to. I didn't hear from anyone. Maybe my number got lost. The atmosphere in the shelter began to change for the worst. I needed to leave the shelter as soon as the EPO hearing took place. I called the church and left a message with my phone number. I was hoping they could help some with the cost of securing my home. It was going to cost less than one hundred dollars. I called the pastor's house a couple days later and left a message with an adult family member. They didn't know what I wanted other than a call back. After three attempts to reach out for help, I gave up. I was hurt, but not crushed. My paycheck was able to pay for the alarms. If I had a little more money for securing my home, I probably would have slept better in a safer home. Imagine this, deposits to turn on utilities, no furniture other than a baby bed and toddler bed, mildew in the carpet, very little clothing, no toiletries, or cleaning supplies…It was expensive moving from the shelter. Around the time of the court date, we stayed with my parents for six days. This allowed me to get the house livable. Child support started that week. My pastor from my "pre-leaving" church called shortly after the day we went to court. At first, I thought after three weeks, he was concerned about us. He actually said he was concerned about making the necessary decisions regarding my husband's job. He needed to know why I left. He did not ask if the children and I were okay. He did ask if there was physical abuse. He said he was faced with a difficult decision. He said if I needed anything to let him know. His biggest concern was, "How long to you think this will take? A week or two?" I told him I did not know, but it must be safe for us to return to the same home. I said that a couple times because he blew it off. Anyway, no compassion. He also told Steve what I had told him in confidentiality. He did know I left only because of the abuse and I wanted to reconcile in a healthy marriage. He tried to make me feel bad for allowing the protection order to continue. He said he has a youth minister with a warrant out on him. That comment was not untrue, but it was the lack of compassion and disbelief that surrounded it that bothered me. My pastor knew I only worked part-time and had two children to support. Maybe he would surprise me. Seven months later, I'm glad I didn't hold my breath. I believed the first time I heard him preach he was abusive to his wife. It was a gut feeling. I think I was right.

In the last seven months, I have gotten phone calls from three Christians we knew mutually. One was a lady from a previous church about 600 miles away. She said Steve called and told her I left and took the kids for no reason. She wanted to know why. She was very straightforward in the way she asked. I figured if Steve thought he had the right to call someone that far away to tell them I left for no reason, I wasn't going to allow them to think I was that kind of person. I told her he was abusive and that was my reason. She was supportive and believed me right away. She did admit she did not see it coming. A friend of Steve's from seminary called me to tell me I needed to be counseling with Steve. Steve was a changed man now an sorry. I didn't feel very well when I got off the phone him. He wasn't getting 3-20 harassing phone calls everyday from Steve. How could he know Steve was "changed" when he didn't know anything was wrong in the first place? Anyway, for us to start counseling at that point, I would have had to drop the protection order. He violated the protection order daily. What would he do if it didn't exist? I got 2 or 3 calls from the music minister's wife from Steve's church. She told me to get over it and to start talking with him more. She was very judgmental and spoke about how she used to get upset with her husband for different things, but they got past that. She admitted her husband was never abusive and had never threatened her life. Her situation was totally different from mine. My husband was <u>still</u> being verbally abusive to me when we met at the police department for switching off the children for visitation. Of course, in her eyes, I was in sin. At least it sounded like that was what she was trying to get me to see. I think she really thought she was doing the right thing by pointing out my "sin". In one of our conversations, she told me someone at church told her, "Pray for Steve. Susan is having an affair." She said she nailed them to the floor. She defended me. I believe good intentions were behind her words and actions. Her helpfulness was very unhelpful and frustrating. I wish she could have heard herself. That is the negative side. Here are some of the positive things that happened. My neighbor (a youth minister's wife) called after dark on Christmas Eve. They wanted to come over. They brought the kids each a toy and a sweater for me. I wanted to cry! When I got the flu, my neighbor mowed my grass. I also used their washer and dryer a couple of times. The education minister (from Steve's church) and his wife sent the kids a couple of gifts for Christmas. I called her to say thank you. We planned to meet sometime while her husband was on a mission trip. She didn't call like she said she would. Maybe she felt awkward. I was glad she thought of us for Christmas. I have two other Christian friends who have continued to encourage me. I don't talk to them frequently because of busy lifestyles,

but they have been wonderful to me. I have received no support (other than those couple of gifts at Christmas) from Steve's church. I attended that church for almost eleven months before leaving my husband. One would think that a church would respond differently. I am okay. God has provided emotionally and materially. However, it could have been much easier with some help. What about the next woman they encounter? I wish their eyes would open.

I've heard stories of women being evicted from their homes because they didn't mow the grass or had the utilities disconnected (lack of money). Maybe her kids' clothes don't fit correctly. Maybe her car is broken down in her driveway and now she is missing work. Don't look down on her. Don't point your finger. Give her a hand. She probably doesn't have much money. She probably doesn't have the "staples" in her home like you do. You open a drawer and find a screwdriver. She opens the drawer and thinks, "I have to <u>buy</u> a screwdriver." Here are some ideas to help.

- Watch out for her. Check on her if you are concerned.
- Offer to watch her children a couple hours per week.
- Let her know you have had problems with ants (if applicable) and offer to spray her baseboards for bugs. She probably doesn't own bug spray.
- Help her change door locks.
- Let her talk and/or cry.
- Invite her to your home. At this point, she may have few friends and although she may not feel "alone", she probably gets lonely.
- Invite her over for holidays. Adopt her into your family.
- Let her borrow your lawn mower or offer to cut her grass. A couple days ago, I was cutting my grass. My children were supposed to be napping. I had to stop the mower at least six times to tell them to go back to bed. She really could use some help sometimes with the simplest tasks.
- Share your washer and dryer once a week or month.

- If she has car trouble, fix it if you are able.
- If she does not have a vehicle, think about how you may be able to help with transportation.
- Help her with home repairs if you are able.
- Mail cash or gift certificates with a note to tell her God loves her.
- Have a house warming party. Maybe families can go in together on things like vacuum cleaners and microwaves.
- Be her friend.
- Give her clothes or groceries once in a while. If she is frugal like me, she probably won't buy clothes unless she has to. She probably only buys necessities at the grocery store. Her family would love to get snack foods and other non-necessity items.
- If you have any skills or services you can offer, it would be a wonderful way to bless her. Can you sew, cut hair, make toys, baby-sit, grow vegetables...Are you a doctor, dentist, lawyer, counselor, plumber...
- Pray for her. Even after leaving, she probably still has a fairly high level of stress. Stress may zap her energy. Pray for her health, both physical and mental.
- Let her know she can call you for help at anytime.

Be creative. It will be fun and she will be encouraged to see God's children helping God's child. You will be glad you did.

God Speaks

Many abusive men twist and distort the scripture. Some pastors will do the same exact thing when a battered woman reaches out to them for spiritual counsel. Almost all ministers will agree that God hates divorce. Some ministers will down play that God hates violence. (I'm not referring to a nation defending itself or personal self defense.) A pastor may make these suggestions:

- Be more submissive.
- Pray more.
- Forgive him and go home.
- Be a better wife, cook, housekeeper, etc...
- Stop making him angry.
- Ask what you did to make him so angry.

He may even accuse her of lying and scold her or accuse her of being unfaithful without reason. This is not a Godly response. She needs to find help elsewhere. I know of some wonderful pastors that offer Godly counsel. She needs to be directed to someone similar.

God hates divorce. The Bible says so in Malachi. This is true. Look deeper.

Malachi 2:13-16

13 Another thing you do: You flood the Lord's altar with tears. You weep and wail because he no longer pays attention to your offerings or accepts them with pleasure from your hands. 14 You ask, "Why?" It is because the Lord is acting as the witness between you and the wife of your youth, because you have broken faith with her, though she is your partner, the wife of your marriage covenant. 15 Has not the Lord made them one? In flesh and spirit they are his. And why one? Because he was seeking godly offspring. So guard yourself in your spirit, and do not break faith with the wife of your youth. 16 "I hate divorce," says the Lord God of Israel, "and I hate a man's covering himself with violence as well as with his garment," says the Lord Almighty. So guard yourself in your spirit, and do not break faith.

That is interesting. God actually hates the act of a man being violent with his wife also. The New International Version (NIV) contains a foot note for verse 16. "Or his wife", it states. It would read like this with the footnote:

16 "I hate divorce," says the Lord God of Israel, "and I hate a man's covering himself [or his wife] with violence as well as with his garment," says the Lord Almighty. So guard yourself in your spirit, and do not break faith.

The NIV talks about "breaking faith". This is talking about being violent or harsh. In the New King James Version (and some other versions) you will see the word "treacherous".

Malachi Chapter 2 (NKJV)

1 **"And now, O priests, this commandment is for you. 2 If you will not hear, And if you will not take it to heart, To give glory to My name," Says the Lord of hosts, "I will send a curse upon you, And I will curse your blessings. Yes, I have** cursed them already, Because you do not take it to heart. *3* "Behold, I will rebuke your descendants And spread refuse on your faces, The refuse of your solemn feasts; And one will take you away with it. *4* Then you shall know that I have sent this commandment to you, That My covenant with Levi may continue," Says the Lord of hosts. *5* "My covenant was with him, one of life and peace, And I gave them to him that he might fear Me; So he feared Me And was reverent before My name. *6* The law of truth [F3] was in his mouth, And injustice was not found on his lips. He walked with Me in peace and equity, And turned many away from iniquity. *7* "For the lips of a priest should keep knowledge, And people should seek the law from his mouth; For he is the messenger of the Lord of hosts. *8* But you have departed from the way; You have caused many to stumble at the law. You have corrupted the covenant of Levi," Says the Lord of hosts. *9* "Therefore I also have made you contemptible and base Before all the people, Because you have not kept My ways But have shown partiality in the law."

10 Have we not all one Father? Has not one God created us? Why do we deal treacherously with one another By profaning the covenant of the fathers? *11* Judah has dealt treacherously, And an abomination has been committed in Israel and in Jerusalem, For Judah has profaned The Lord's holy institution which He loves: He has married the daughter of a foreign god. *12* May the Lord cut off from the tents of Jacob The man who does this, being awake and aware, [F4] Yet who brings an offering to the Lord of hosts! *13* And this is the second thing you do: You cover the altar of the Lord with tears, With weeping and crying; So He does not regard the offering anymore, Nor receive it with goodwill from your hands. *14* Yet you say, "For what reason?" Because the Lord has been witness Between you and the wife of your youth, With whom you have dealt treacherously; Yet she is your companion And your wife by covenant. *15* But did He not make them one, Having a remnant of the Spirit? And why one? He seeks godly offspring. Therefore take heed to your spirit, And let none deal treacherously with the wife of his youth. *16* "For the Lord God of Israel says That He hates divorce, For it covers one's garment with violence," Says the Lord of hosts. "Therefore take heed to your spirit, That you do not deal treacherously." *17* You have wearied the Lord with your words; Yet you say, "In what way have we wearied Him?" In that you say, "Everyone who does evil Is good in the sight of the Lord, And He delights in them," Or, "Where is the God of justice?"

FOOTNOTES:
F3: *Or true instruction*
F4: *Talmud and Vulgate read teacher and student.*

God uses the word "treacherous" five times. Do we have the right to believe that it is not acceptable behavior to act treacherously towards another person? YES, we do! It is even more important for a husband to not deal with his wife in a treacherous or harsh manner. Actions <u>and</u> words can be used in a treacherous way. It is ungodly and definitely falls under the category of sin. Both violence and adultery would be unfaithfulness to the marriage covenant.

1 Peter

3:7

Husbands, in the same way be considerate as you live with your wives, and treat them with respect as the weaker partner and as heirs with you of the gracious gift of life, so that nothing will hinder your prayers.

3:8

Finally, all of you, live in harmony with one another; be sympathetic, love as brothers, be compassionate and humble.

3:9

Do not repay evil with evil or insult with insult, but with blessing, because to this you were called so that you may inherit a blessing.

3:10

For, "Whoever would love life and see good days must keep his tongue from evil and his lips from deceitful speech.

3:11

He must turn from evil and do good; he must seek peace and pursue it.

3:12

For the eyes of the Lord are on the righteous and his ears are attentive to their prayer, but the face of the Lord is against those who do evil."

1. She is not "lesser" than her husband. Men typically have more physical strength than women. Therefore, he should protect her with his masculine body God gave him.
2. An abusive husband's prayers will be hindered.

Proverbs 11:29

He who brings trouble on his family will inherit only wind, and the fool will be servant to the wise.

Violence definitely troubles a home. During the time this was written, it was easier to understand because of their culture. As they harvested the fields, the wind would sometimes blow away what they had worked for all day. Their grain would be taken away by the wind.

The whole submission thing

Ephesians 5:21-29

5:21
Submit to one another out of reverence for Christ.

5:22
Wives, submit to your husbands as to the Lord.

5:23
For the husband is the head of the wife as Christ is the head of the church, his body, of which he is the Savior.

5:24
Now as the church submits to Christ, so also wives should submit to their husbands in everything.

5:25
Husbands, love your wives, just as Christ loved the church and gave himself up for her

5:26
to make her holy, cleansing her by the washing with water through the word,

5:27

and to present her to himself as a radiant church, without stain or wrinkle or any other blemish, but holy and blameless.

5:28

In this same way, husbands ought to love their wives as their own bodies. He who loves his wife loves himself.

5:29

After all, no one ever hated his own body, but he feeds and cares for it, just as Christ does the church —

Verse 21 is speaking of a mutual submission and respect between all brothers and sisters in Christ, including husbands and wives. The husband is not "the boss." He should not dominate. There will be times when he needs to make decisions. If the issue affects his wife or family, a wise husband will consult with his wife. He should try to wait to make the decision until they have come to an agreement. Nor is she his inferior personal servant. They are to work as a team. She is to nurture him, as he is to take care of her as a servant-leader should. While Jesus walked the earth, He displayed servant leadership. He served others. He was gentle, compassionate, humble, and protective over the oppressed... He was not prideful, harsh, demanding, critical, or abusive in any way. The overall character of Christ is a model of how a man should treat his family. Why would someone think they have the right to terrorize their family because they are the "leader of this home"? It is not Biblical at all. The character of Christ tells me a man should be willing to do what it takes to protect his wife physically and emotionally. He should be willing to help with housework, change diapers, lay down his life to protect his family, provide for his family the best he can, be gentle, be aware of his family's needs, give his wife some quiet or fun time, comfort her (even if the issue seems silly to him), love and cherish her...

Read Rocking the Roles by Robert Lewis and William Hendricks for an excellent job description for men and women of God.

Mark 10:44

and whoever wants to be first must be slave of all.

Matthew 20

20:25

Jesus called them together and said, "You know that the rulers of the Gentiles lord it over them, and their high offi͗ als exercise authority over them.

20:26

Not so with you. Instead, whoever wants to become great among you must be your servant,

Philippians 2:4

Each of you should look not only to your own interests, but also to the interests of others.

Matthew 23:10

Nor are you to be called 'teacher,' for you have one Teacher, the Christ

God's way is a servant type of leadership. We must learn from the Teacher. This is not the world's style. But, it is the style of the One who created the world.

1 Corinthians 7

7:3

The husband should fulfill his marital duty to his wife, and likewise the wife to her husband.

7:4

The wife's body does not belong to her alone but also to her husband. In the same way, the husband's body does not belong to him alone but also to his wife.

This does not give a husband right to force his wife sexually. Marriage does not justify rape. If she is uncomfortable (physically or mentally), frightened or not wanting sex or a certain type of sexual activity, she has the right to say no. He may use manipulation or physical force to get what he wants. This is just another form of abuse. Sex between married couples is supposed to be something beautiful, not something that makes her physically sick to her stomach. Many batterers want sex immediately after he explodes. This is a way for him to reclaim his victim. Saying "no" is not an option for her. I attended a women's meeting and brought up the sex issue. After being separated for seven months, I began to have a new awareness of my personal experience in that area. Going by the healthy boundary I just gave (where she should be able to say "no"), I was a victim of sexual violence. This thought was not put in my head by anyone or anything. God probably revealed it to me at that point because I was strong enough to handle it. One night, some memories of manipulation and control in our bedroom began to surface. As I opened up to the other women, their heads began to nod. Saying "no" was not an option for any of us. We knew the consequences. I believe sexual abuse is the most difficult to overcome emotionally. I would then place verbal and physical on the list.

1 Corinthians

3:16

Don't you know that you yourselves are God's temple and that God's Spirit lives in you?

3:17

If anyone destroys God's temple, God will destroy him; for God's temple is sacred, and you are that temple.

God wants us to be safe. He does not wink when His child is harmed.

Proverbs 22:6

Train a child in the way he should go, and when he is old he will not turn from it.

Ephesians 6:4

Fathers, do not exasperate your children; instead, bring them up in the training and instruction of the Lord.

"Instruction in the Lord" would also include providing a safe environment both physically and mentally. This scripture should encourage a woman in an unhealthy relationship to take action for the sake of her children. They will live what they learn by observation. This should also convict a violent man to control his actions around his children.

Luke 17:2

It would be better for him to be thrown into the sea with a millstone tied around his neck than for him to cause one of these little ones to sin.

Matthew 18

18:5 "And whoever welcomes a little child like this in my name welcomes me.

18:6 But if anyone causes one of these little ones who believe in me to sin, it would be better for him to have a large millstone hung around his neck and to be drowned in the depths of the sea.

18:7 "Woe to the world because of the things that cause people to sin! Such things must come, but woe to the man through whom they come!

18:8 If your hand or your foot causes you to sin, cut it off and throw it away. It is better for you to enter life maimed or crippled than to have two hands or two feet and be thrown into eternal fire.

This sounds serious. It is. What would make a child stumble faster than the confusion and fear that comes from having a violent father?

2 Timothy

3:1 But mark this: There will be terrible times in the last days.

3:2 People will be lovers of themselves, lovers of money, boastful, proud, abusive, disobedient to their parents, ungrateful, unholy,

3:3 without love, unforgiving, slanderous, without self-control, brutal, not lovers of the good,

3:4 treacherous, rash, conceited, lovers of pleasure rather than lovers of God—

3:5 having a form of godliness but denying its power. Have nothing to do with them.

1 John 1

1:5 This is the message we have heard from him and declare to you: God is light; in him there is no darkness at all.

1:6 If we claim to have fellowship with him yet walk in the darkness, we lie and do not live by the truth.

1:7 But if we walk in the light, as he is in the light, we have fellowship with one another, and the blood of Jesus, his Son, purifies us from all sin.

Don't be fooled. This may be someone currently in the church or an abuser putting on a religious mask to sway his partner to come back or to sway the courts.

Luke 6

6:27

> **"But I tell you who hear me: Love your enemies, do good to those who hate you,**

6:28

> **bless those who curse you, pray for those who mistreat you.**

6:29

If someone strikes you on one cheek, turn to him the other also. If someone takes your cloak, do not stop him from taking your tunic.

Romans 12

12:9

Love must be sincere. Hate what is evil; cling to what is good.

12:10

Be devoted to one another in brotherly love. Honor one another above yourselves.

12:11

Never be lacking in zeal, but keep your spiritual fervor, serving the Lord.

12:12

Be joyful in hope, patient in affliction, faithful in prayer.

12:13

Share with God's people who are in need. Practice hospitality.

12:14

Bless those who persecute you; bless and do not curse.

12:15

Rejoice with those who rejoice; mourn with those who mourn.

12:16

> Live in harmony with one another. Do not be proud, but be willing to associate with people of low position. Do not be conceited.

12:17

> Do not repay anyone evil for evil. Be careful to do what is right in the eyes of everybody.

12:18

> If it is possible, as far as it depends on you, live at peace with everyone.

12:19

> Do not take revenge, my friends, but leave room for God's wrath, for it is written: "It is mine to avenge; I will repay," says the Lord.

She should not fight fire with fire. She does have the right and justification to leave and go to safety. When she leaves, God will take care of her. The word of God states that and my experience is evidence.

Matthew 6

6:25

> "Therefore I tell you, do not worry about your life, what you will eat or drink; or about your body, what you will wear. Is not life more important than food, and the body more important than clothes?

6:26

> Look at the birds of the air; they do not sow or reap or store away in barns, and yet your heavenly Father feeds them. Are you not much more valuable than they?

6:27

Who of you by worrying can add a single hour to his life?

6:28

"And why do you worry about clothes? See how the lilies of the field grow. They do not labor or spin.

6:29

Yet I tell you that not even Solomon in all his splendor was dressed like one of these.

6:30

If that is how God clothes the grass of the field, which is here today and tomorrow is thrown into the fire, will he not much more clothe you, O you of little faith?

6:31

So do not worry, saying, 'What shall we eat?' or 'What shall we drink?' or 'What shall we wear?'

6:32

For the pagans run after all these things, and your heavenly Father knows that you need them.

6:33

But seek first his kingdom and his righteousness, and all these things will be given to you as well.

6:34

Therefore do not worry about tomorrow, for tomorrow will worry about itself. Each day has enough trouble of its own.

Psalms

59:16

But I will sing of your strength, in the morning I will sing of your love; for you are my fortress, my refuge in times of trouble.

59:17

O my Strength, I sing praise to you; you, O God, are my fortress, my loving God.

Matthew 7

7:7

"Ask and it will be given to you; seek and you will find; knock and the door will be opened to you.

7:8

For everyone who asks receives; he who seeks finds; and to him who knocks, the door will be opened.

2 Corinthians 5:7

We live by faith, not by sight.

Philippians 4:13

I can do everything through him who gives me strength.

Psalms 41

41:1

Blessed is he who has regard for the weak; the Lord delivers him in times of trouble.

41:2

The Lord will protect him and preserve his life; he will bless him in the land and not surrender him to the desire of his foes.

41:3

The Lord will sustain him on his sickbed and restore him from his bed of illness.

John 10:10

The thief comes only to steal and kill and destroy; I have come that they may have life, and have it to the full.

1 John 5

5:14

This is the confidence we have in approaching God: that if we ask anything according to his will, he hears us.

God does not condone out of control violence.

Colossians 3:19

Husbands, love your wives and do not be harsh with them.

Proverbs 10

10:9

The man of integrity walks securely, but he who takes crooked paths will be found out.

James 1

1:19
My dear brothers, take note of this: Everyone should be quick to listen, slow to speak and slow to become angry,

Proverbs 13

13:17
A wicked messenger falls into trouble, but a trustworthy envoy brings healing.

13:18
He who ignores discipline comes to poverty and shame, but whoever heeds correction is honored.

Proverbs 14

14:16
A wise man fears the Lord and shuns evil, but a fool is hotheaded and reckless.

14:17
A quick-tempered man does foolish things, and a crafty man is hated.

Proverbs 10:11
The mouth of the righteous is a fountain of life, but violence overwhelms the mouth of the wicked.

Proverbs 16:32
Better a patient man than a warrior, a man who controls his temper than one who takes a city.

Proverbs 14:29

A patient man has great understanding, but a quick-tempered man displays folly.

Proverbs 21:7

The violence of the wicked will drag them away, for they refuse to do what is right.

Here are some other scriptures you may find helpful.

Psalms 22:24

For he has not despised or disdained the suffering of the afflicted one; he has not hidden his face from him but has listened to his cry for help.

Psalms 118

118:5

In my anguish I cried to the Lord, and he answered by setting me free.

118:6

The Lord is with me; I will not be afraid. What can man do to me?

118:7

The Lord is with me; he is my helper. I will look in triumph on my enemies.

Psalms 55:22

Cast your cares on the Lord and he will sustain you; he will never let the righteous fall.

Psalms 3

3:1

O Lord, how many are my foes! How many rise up against me!

3:2

Many are saying of me, "God will not deliver him." Selah

3:3

But you are a shield around me, O Lord; you bestow glory on me and lift up my head.

3:4

To the Lord I cry aloud, and he answers me from his holy hill. Selah

3:5

I lie down and sleep; I wake again, because the Lord sustains me.

Psalms 12:5

"Because of the oppression of the weak and the groaning of the needy, I will now arise," says the Lord. "I will protect them from those who malign them."

Psalms 18

18:40

You made my enemies turn their backs in flight, and I destroyed my foes.

18:41

> They cried for help, but there was no one to save them —
> to the Lord, but he did not answer.

18:42

> I beat them as fine as dust borne on the wind; I poured
> them out like mud in the streets.

18:43

> You have delivered me from the attacks of the people;
> you have made me the head of nations; people I did not
> know are subject to me.

18:44

> As soon as they hear me, they obey me; foreigners cringe
> before me.

18:45

> They all lose heart; they come trembling from their
> strongholds.

18:46

> The Lord lives! Praise be to my Rock! Exalted be God
> my Savior!

18:47

> He is the God who avenges me, who subdues nations
> under me,

18:48

> who saves me from my enemies. You exalted me above
> my foes; from violent men you rescued me.

Psalms 31:8

You have not handed me over to the enemy but have set my feet in a spacious place.

Psalms 84

84:3

Even the sparrow has found a home, and the swallow a nest for herself, where she may have her young— a place near your altar, O Lord Almighty, my King and my God.

84:4

Blessed are those who dwell in your house; they are ever praising you. Selah

Psalms 140:4

Keep me, O Lord, from the hands of the wicked; protect me from men of violence who plan to trip my feet.

Proverbs 18:10

The name of the Lord is a strong tower; the righteous run to it and are safe.

Psalms 144:7

Reach down your hand from on high; deliver me and rescue me from the mighty waters, from the hands of foreigners

Proverbs 27:12

The prudent see danger and take refuge, but the simple keep going and suffer for it.

Philippians 4

4:6

Do not be anxious about anything, but in everything, by prayer and petition, with thanksgiving, present your requests to God.

4:7

And the peace of God, which transcends all understanding, will guard your hearts and your minds in Christ Jesus.

1 Peter 5

5:6

Humble yourselves, therefore, under God's mighty hand, that he may lift you up in due time.

5:7

Cast all your anxiety on him because he cares for you.

You may find Psalms 140, 27, 23, and 55 encouraging.
Proverbs contains much wisdom. Read Proverbs 3:25-26, 3:31-35, 13:2, 18:1, and 29:9.

You Are Not Alone

It seems to be across the board. Abuse victims feel alone and isolated with no one to turn to. Some are more isolated than others. She wants to know she is not alone. Statistics that are documented and with evidence behind them may show 1 in 5 women will be victims. Independent studies where people are polled with the "raise your hand" method show 40-50% of women may be abused. Whichever is correct, it is happening too much. These are not just numbers. They are precious women and children that God created. And their lives are being turned upside down. They are afraid and feel completely alone. For the first couple of months after I left my husband, it helped to hear other women's stories. Why? It confirmed that I was not the only one. It did not bring joy to know others had suffered, but it empowered me to know that I would also get past that stage in my life. I spoke to a woman recently who left her husband five months ago. She still just needed to hear she was not alone. She still felt the need to assure me she was telling the truth. She said it felt wonderful to know other women would encourage her, listen to her, and at times be a voice for her when she didn't have the strength to speak. As she kept saying she was not lying, she said she will be in contact with her congressman about changing some ridiculous laws her state had about visitation. She said she didn't see herself as human yet. She would not pray for herself yet. BUT, the woman had a fire in her and was ready to take on the state to improve laws that should protect her children. I told her to go for it. She was very passionate about making a difference. At the same time, she wanted someone to stand by her so she could know she was not alone. She had strength for her children, but not for herself.

As I have been growing back into myself again, I'm much more vocal about abuse. As I say more, other women are telling me they are also survivors or currently in an unhealthy situation. It encourages me to meet women whose lives seem completely rebuilt. I was "alone" when I lived in a violent home. Now "alone" does not happen any longer because God has had me cross paths with so many women who had the same title to their life, but only the details were different. As I'm still rebuilding my life, and probably will be for quite awhile, it brings me joy to help others know they are not alone any longer and that life does get better. We must lean on Jesus for our strength. He does know what we are going through. Two thousand years ago, as He hung on the cross, He carried the weight of our sin, shame, sickness… He felt the burden of abuse, terror, failure and so on. He knows how it feels and wants us to have a better life. He wants us to become healthy both mentally and physically. As I felt completely alone while living with my husband, I wasn't. My God was with me the whole time. Did it feel like it? Not usually, but looking back I see Him. I still am bothered by the fact that my two beautiful children suffered. I want this whole experience to be turned into something that will give God the glory. I want my children to know that sometimes life is hard, but our God will lift us up in His loving hands. I don't want any more bad experiences for my children or myself. I want to be able to tell them when they are older about our life. I want to tell them few details about the situation, but lots of details about how God took care of us.

If you are in an unhealthy relationship, YOU ARE NOT ALONE. Help is out there. You must let someone know. Tell someone you can trust or call a crisis line. You need to know what resources are available in your community. Your local police department probably has access to that information. You are not the only woman to experience abuse from your husband. Find other women who have escaped their relationships to speak with about your situation. It will help you to know that life does get easier. The sooner you can begin to rebuild, the better.

I was unable to go to support meetings and counseling before I left. Talking on the phone to a counselor really helped me to feel less alone. Moving into a shelter also had some emotional benefits. In some ways, I felt an instant bond with the other women staying there. We had the common experience of abuse. The severity of the abuse varied. The types of scars varied. What we had in common was a fear of a man we once thought would protect us, not hurt us. I was in the shelter when it really clicked. I'm not the only one. My head knew it before, but at the shelter, my heart figured out that truth. I asked my new acquaintances to remind me I did the right thing by leaving. As they reminded me I did the right thing, my anxiousness slowly became peace. I did it! I was safe! My children were safe and I did the right thing!

Conclusion

Now that my "brochure" is complete, here is the update. Six months ago when I picked up a pen, it was to compile information into a little brochure to help educate pastors and others in leadership positions within the church. Since I started writing, a lot of healing has taken place in my life. My faith has grown along with my desire to serve God in a way that will help other women. I have had several opportunities to reach out to others and believe it is part of His plan for my life. I guess I can be useful even though my situation is still up in the air.

I left my husband nine months ago. Yes, he is still the youth pastor at the same church. Jaws tend to drop when people hear that. I believe it is wrong that he is still teaching, but I'm not surprised. Maybe the church isn't aware of the Biblical qualifications of an elder. Maybe they just don't care (that's my guess). The harassing phone calls slowed down significantly after I let the police know what he was doing. Once in a while, he gets out of control or manipulative on the phone, or when we meet at the police station for visitation exchanges. Regardless, it is much more peaceful than before I decided to enforce the legal protection my community offered. I am very cautious in many ways still. I'm not as fearful every time a bug flies into my windows at night. I sleep with a land-line phone, cell phone, and self defense spray in arms reach many nights. Training in self-defense has also helped me to feel like less of a target.

My husband still gets to me sometimes. I'm much stronger now than nine months ago. I get most upset when he uses the children. He is angry that he only sees them twice weekly. He threatens to take legal action to get the children. Then he tells me I should "know" he is a changed man because he hasn't taken me to court. That is just an example. His overall actions and words have me convinced of the exact opposite. He is still an abuser. In two weeks, he will be finished with the anger management classes. After that, we will begin marriage counseling. He has been very pushy and demanding about getting me into counseling with him. I am agreeing to it because nine months ago, I agreed to it. At the time, the court would not allow. I agree with the decision the court had made. In two weeks it will be legal to attend counseling together. Other than that, the protection order will stay in effect. I'm a little nervous about the counseling, but if it gets too bad, I have the right to decide if I want to go back. It is something I feel I need to give a chance. I don't want to look back in twenty years and wish I would have tried harder.

My children and I have begun living again. We attend a wonderful church where I attend counseling every other week with a very insightful Christian counselor. We go to the park, play in the yard, and let the housework wait sometimes. We even go to the local airport to watch the planes. In the last month or two, I've talked more about my situation in my small group. They pray for us and are encouragers. Another single mom has agreed to kind of take me under her wing. I asked her for some wisdom because my four year old son is really struggling. He has a lot of anger. In the last month, he punched the storm door and broke the glass. He has really been aggressive. Today, he threw a kitchen chair and punched me. I am being very firm with him when he acts out. It looks like it may take a while to reroute the way he expresses anger. He is a very loving and sensitive child. His outbursts have got to stop. My daughter usually has trouble sleeping the night after she has been with her dad. For the most part, she is doing well.

Sometimes I get lonely, but loneliness is much better than what went on when my husband lived with us. If Steve never gets better, I don't see myself dating anytime in the next several years. It was just too bad of an experience to chance it happening again while Isaac and Renee are small. Until something changes, I will be content being a married, single mom. My job is very stressful, but I'm able to support my family by only working part-time. I feel very blessed to be able to spend so much time as a stay at home mom. Of course money is tight. It is worth the sacrifice. After they have been with their dad, Isaac and Renee typically show signs of what type of mood they saw in him. When he is in a calm stage, so are they. When he is not, neither are they. I wish my conclusion was: And they lived happily ever after together. I don't know what the future holds. I do know that living in a violent home again is not an option for us.

I can be contacted by phone or email.
Susangreenfield1@hotmail.com
(940)452-3279

Statistics

National Coalition Against Domestic Violence:

- Studies have found that child abuse occurs in up to 70% of families that experience
  domestic violence.
- One study revealed that recent exposure to violence in the home was a significant factor in predicting a child's violent behavior.
- Fathers who batter the mothers of their children, are twice as likely to seek sole custody of their children.
- Despite the perception that mothers always win custody cases, studies show that fathers who contest custody win sole or joint custody in 40-70% of cases.

American Institute on Domestic Violence:

- Domestic violence is the leading cause of injury to women.
- Women are more likely to be attacked by someone they know rather than by a stranger.
- Battered workers-
    96% experience problems at work due to abuse
    74% are harassed while at work by their abusers
    54% miss entire days of work
    56% are late to work
    28% leave work early

- Homicide is the leading cause of death for women in the workplace.

Crimes Against Children Research Center:

- For 1999, the second National Incidence Study of Missing, Abducted, Runaway, and Thrownaway Children estimated that 203,900 children had experienced a family abduction.
- 44% of family abducted children were younger than age 6.
- Biological fathers were the most frequent abductor.

Hammer,H.,Finkelhor, D., & Sedlak, A. (2000). Children abducted by family members: National estimated and Characteristics. <u>Juvenile Justice Bulletin</u>. Washington, DC: Office of Juvenile Justiice and Delinquency Prevention.

Resources

Bancroft, Lundy. <u>Why does he do that? Inside the minds of angry and controlling men</u> 143-147

Hegstrom, Paul. <u>Broken children, grown up pain</u>

Power and Control Wheel developed by the Domestic Abuse Intervention Project. Duluth, MD

Checklists for Identifying Abuse are a modified version of non-copyrighted material given to shelter residents at a specific shelter.

All Scripture is taken from the New International Version of the <u>Bible</u> unless otherwise noted. Copyright © 1973, 1978, 1984 by International Bible Society.

New King James Version. Copyright © 1992 by Thomas Nelson, Inc.

Resources are also noted within text.

LaVergne, TN USA
20 January 2010
170594LV00005B/3/A